What They're Saying about Get-Real Selling

"There are many, many competent sales professionals. Reading and referring to this book, however, will make you a consciously competent sales professional, giving you a real competitive advantage in the market."

SCOTT COLLINS, Senior Vice President of Sales, Harcourt

"The only thing easier than reading this book is the success you will find from using these techniques for becoming a true consultative sales professional. By far the most valuable book I've ever read about becoming the total solutions provider for your clients."

GARY F. WEBER, Senior Sales Advisor, Aurora Casket Company

"The secrets in this book guided me in successfully transforming a six hundred-person sales organization. The examples and insights are real world and can be put into action today and every day after. It should be on every sales executive's book shelf."

RON LAMB, Vice President of Sales, Reynolds & Reynolds

"As a profession, sales is moving from a reliance on relationships and instinct to a profession that requires significantly more science. All sales professionals need to constantly update and hone their skills. This book captures the science you need to be a sales professional in one easy read."

TOM OGBURN, Vice President, LexisNexis Government Sales

"The book has stayed with me. Not just Keith's and Michael's approach to sales, but the passion and the conviction of their beliefs about the approach. I felt cheated that, even though I grew up in sales, I never really got it the way I did after I read *Get-Real Selling*."

JUDIE KNOERLE, President, daK and Company

Dedications

I am extremely beholden to the sales greats that have come before me in my business career. They have no idea how much they have influenced my skills, knowledge, beliefs, and success. Mert, Hunter, Fred, Lou, Brian, and my Irondog buddies, I hope you know how much you have shaped me and my career. Michael Boland, my co-author and business partner, also tops my list of greats who have influenced my professional development. There would be no *Get-Real Selling* without this relentless sales professional.

From a personal perspective, all of my work is inspired by the great family that surrounds my every thought. My sons Matt, Ryan, and AJ inspire effort, discipline, and finding fun in all things I do. Beth and Laura, my daughters-in-law, have brought much-needed female perspectives, love, and laughter to our lives. Our grandchildren, Nathan and Paige, are joys who keep us young. My parents, Dean and Mary, are joyous, solid people who gave me a firm foundation on which to grow. Finally, my wife Judy is the core of my inspiration with her love, compassion for work, and self-discipline. With her constant focus on the family as our Number One priority, she is at the heart of what is truly Real. Thanks to one and all.

Keith Hawk

I learned early in my life to associate with those who are best in class, and to help others become the same. It started with my upbringing back in Frog Hollow, Pennsylvania, where my parents Joe and Renee instilled the gifts of faith, family, love, and hard work in my six brothers and sisters and me. My professional growth was shaped by mentors such as Carlos, Page, Ed, David, and Bob, who afforded me the opportunity to grow on the international stage. Thanks also to my associates at Wilson Learning and Performance Technologies, who for 25 years set the standards for excellence, and to my clients, who required my firm to continuously reinvent itself. I am also indebted to my co-author and partner Keith Hawk, who is the consummate sales professional, leader, family man, and most importantly, my friend.

I am grateful to my daughters, who all grew up in Performance Technologies and contributed to its success, and to our close family - daughters, sons-in-law, and grandchildren - all of whom are one another's best friend. Finally I am eternally grateful to my wife Emilee, whose unconditional love and support has sustained us through our epic journey. She is truly the greatest get-real sale of my life!

Michael P. Boland

Get-Real Selling

Your personal coach for **REAL** sales excellence

Keith Hawk

Michael Boland

The models listed below are proprietary to Wilson Learning Corporation and are referenced herein by permission: Ben Duffy, Purpose Process, Payoff; Account Behavior Spectrum; Discovery; Solution-Advantage-Benefit; Social Style; Credibility; LSCPA. Task and Personal Motives, Versatility, Consultant and Strategist, Professional Relationship Selling

How to order: Single copies may be ordered online at www.novavistapub.com. In North America, you may phone 503-548-7597. Elsewhere, dial +32-14-21-11-21. Available in bookstores and libraries near you.

ISBN 978-90-77256-17-6
20 19 18 17 16 15 14 13 12 11 10 9 8 7 6 5 4 3 2
Cover design: Wouter Geukens
Editorial: Andrew Karre, Elizabeth Karre
Text design: Layout Sticker
Printed in United States of America

Contents

**Part 3: Hidden Elements of Sales Professionalism that Will
Make You Stand Out from the Rest**

Appendix

Foreword

Let us start by using one of the techniques we recommend in this book. We bet you are wondering, "Who are these guys? And why do they think they have something to say that will help me sell better?" Here's our answer.

We have spent our entire professional lives in the world of selling. We have been on-the-street sales professionals, sales managers, and sales VPs of large corporations. As owners of a business consulting and training firm, we have consulted with hundreds of sales executives and conducted over a thousand seminars on a myriad of selling skills topics. Over the last three decades, we have developed strong, specific opinions on what defines sales and sales-leadership effectiveness. We have learned from great successes and from the occasional disappointment.

We thank you for your interest in getting Real. We want to help you maximize your potential. We want to validate your belief that selling is one of the world's most noble professions, one that truly contributes to society. By definition, salespeople *make things work better* – that is what we DO. People do not buy unless there is something missing or something wrong in their business or their life. As sales professionals, it is our job to discover things that are wrong and make them right with our solutions.

If you are a working sales professional who is intent on becoming more consciously competent, meaning you want to vividly understand what it takes to be great, then this book is for you. If you are interested in cutting through garbage to find specific processes, skills, and tools you can use with enthusiasm and relentless dedication to get measurable results, then this book is for you. It's all about getting Real in sales.

You now know who we are and where we're coming from. We hope we've stirred your curiosity and desire to improve. Let us help you get there with *Get-Real Selling!*

Keith Hawk
Vice President, Client Relations
LexisNexis, Inc.

Michael Boland
President and Founder
Performance Technologies, Inc.

Editor's Note

It's been a pleasure working with Keith Hawk and Michael Boland, two seasoned and successful veterans of sales and sales leadership, on *Get-Real Selling*. It was vitally important to them both that this book really deliver on its promises to you, a sales professional who's thirsty for ways to improve your effectiveness. I hope you'll agree that they've done just that.

Keith and Michael differentiate themselves from authors of books that spend hundreds of pages on broad, high-level *theories*. They prefer to cut to the heart of what it takes to attain greatness in the noble profession of selling. With this in mind, we decided to structure this book in two unique ways:

1. Keep the chapters short and pithy, distilling critical info and experiences into hard-hitting key points. Why waste your time?
2. Illustrate points by describing not only proven, best approaches, but also by flagging common *wrong ways* that salespeople do things – which we dub *Not Real*. So watch for these, marked with this icon:

and learn to avoid doing what salespeople or their managers often think or do incorrectly.

Get ready now to enjoy this fast-reading, meaty book and profit from the experience and insights of two veterans who have dedicated their working lives to the development of sales professionals. If you absorb and practice the processes and techniques that they've developed, you will GET REAL and change your life in sales for the better!

Kathe Grooms
Editor and Publisher
Nova Vista Publishing

Part 1

Setting the Stage: The True Purpose of the Consultative Sales Professional

"My job is to make my customer's businesses run more smoothly, more profitably, and to make their lives better!"

This opening section sets the stage for our point of view that our principle purpose as sales professionals is to enhance the business and the lives of our customers. We define our core fundamentals that begin to paint the picture of *how* we differentiate ourselves as professionals who seek out and solve business problems. We will also clarify the often fuzzy and misunderstood concept of Solutions Selling.

Introduction
How *Get Real* Got Started

Keith and I have been business associates for fifteen years, starting with a client-supplier arrangement that evolved into a business partnership. In 1999, we started kicking around the idea of writing a book on sales but had not yet started it.

In March of 2000, Keith and I were guests at the national sales meeting of one of our newly acquired accounts. Keith was the keynote speaker for about a hundred of the corporate and field sales managers in the organization. His address was positioned to introduce the company's new initiative: installing a consultative sales and coaching process.

Keith was preceded by the president of the company, who came up through the sales ranks himself.

The president spoke first about how important it was for every manager there to be a good sales coach for their teams. He stressed how critical it was for everyone in their organization to be consultative in their approach to customers. He extolled the attributes of effective problem solvers and urged everybody to focus on the needs of their customers and on helping them solve their business problems. This would be their new way of differentiating themselves from their competitors.

Then this leader abruptly shifted his focus to the sales performance of the previous year. Suddenly his tone turned cold. He began to berate his managers for not consistently meeting their sales objectives. He trashed their management skills, attacking the high turnover rate of salespeople and the low rate of new customer acquisition. To our dismay, he urged these managers to use all tactics necessary to bring on new customers, including price and product gimmicks.

The president closed his remarks by threatening to reduce the head count in this management group if sales performance did not improve within the first months of the new fiscal year.

Keith and I stood at the back of the room, stunned by this leader's abrupt

Jekyll-and-Hyde transformation. What a way to warm up the audience for this new consultative sales and coaching philosophy they were about embrace! We turned to each other, and one of us muttered, "Get Real!"

That moment became the genesis for two books, one about selling and one about sales coaching and leadership. We chose to address *Get-Real Selling* first because it is applicable to the entire sales profession and also because it sets the framework for coaching.

Just as this leader demonstrated, salespeople try to do things right, yet they sometimes gravitate to undesirable selling behaviors when under pressure. We examine this tendency, not just by explaining the right way to sell, which we call Real selling, but also by sharing Not Real, wrong-way examples. You may wince in recognition as you read these wake-up calls, but that's a positive first step on the path to conscious competence. Don't beat yourself up – just make changes and you'll see Real, good results.

Our book takes a broad yet pragmatic approach to the world of sales. Each section provides golden nuggets for salespeople, no matter where they are in their sales career.

Part 1 addresses the sales profession. We view sales as a noble calling, so we share experiences and give you specific advice on how to be highly professional when dealing with your customers.

Part 2 focuses on the sales process, with special emphasis on the inter-actions that take place between a salesperson and his or her customers. It starts with targeting whom to call on, then shows how to access and engage prospects and customers, and ends with techniques for successfully closing sales opportunities.

I was very fortunate early in my sales career to have met Larry Wilson and become familiar with his work as a pioneer in the art of Consulta-tive Selling. Through that connection, and from my subsequent 25 years of being affiliated with the Wilson Learning organization, come several of the selling principles described in this book. They reflect his and their sales philosophy.

Part 3 focuses on behind-the-scenes aspects of selling – those key ele-ments that customers don't see but which are required to win new business. We show you how to manage your sales role and responsibilities, regardless of whether you are self-employed or work in a large sales organization.

Finally, Part 4 shows you how to integrate your career in sales with the goal of living life in a supremely fulfilling way.

We hope that you experience a revelation or two and grab helpful ideas from each short chapter. Perhaps you will incorporate them into your already effective repertoire of skills that drive your current success. We hope that they will take you to a higher level of winning and living.

Earlier I mentioned that we believe this book will help people in any phase of their sales career. To test that, we sent our manuscript to a diverse group of sales professionals for comment. Here are a few responses that confirm that this book is not just for sales beginners:

> *I kept regretting that I didn't have this book 25 years ago. It would have saved me from many hard knocks.*
> *Linda Bower, Principal, Human Performance Strategies*

> *My father was one of those old fashioned salesmen – on the road all week, home on the weekends, stressed and worried most of the time. After his stroke at the age of 57, I found one of his old sales manuals in a drawer: 101 Ways to Close a Deal. I so wish someone had handed him Get-Real Selling at the beginning of his career. He would have been more fulfilled and more connected to his family and customers, and at the start of my own sales career I would have found this book.*
> *Judie Knoerlie, President, dAK and Company*

Keith and I are honored that you have chosen to read *Get-Real Selling*. We hope that you find your investment of time and money well spent and that you enjoy huge dividends for the rest of your Real selling life!

Peace,
Michael Boland

1 Sales Is the Greatest Profession

In speaking to groups of business professionals on a regular basis, I often ask them to tell me about their "dream jobs" – jobs they would have if talent, luck, and opportunity were no obstacle. I always get a variety of exciting and sometimes unrealistic responses. I regularly hear of the desire to be professional golfers, flower shop owners, chefs in great restaurants, rock stars, and a wide variety of glamorous roles. When I ask why they are not pursuing these dream jobs, these professionals talk about talent shortfalls, lack of capital, risk aversion, and the pressure of family demands that force them into more common, stable jobs.

I then typically ask this follow-up question: "Within the business world, what would you most like to do?" I do this to get people to be more realistic in their assessment of what they would truly like to do, yet are somehow blocked from doing. Invariably, the number one response is, "I would love to run my own business."

When I probe for the reason why there is such a universal desire to run the show as an entrepreneur, I hear the following replies:

- "I want to be the boss."
- "I want to be compensated based upon *my* work, *my* success."
- "I want greater control over how I spend my day."
- "I do not want to work in a big office environment – I want to be out in the business community with people from other businesses."

I always see lots of excitement and consistency in these responses. Yet the fact remains that most people do not take that step to start their own business. When I probe further for the obstacles to pursuing this business dream, I hear things like:

- "I can't afford to expose my family to the financial risk of losing our money."
- "Who needs the troubles that come from managing the group of employ-

ees I would need if I ran my own business?"

- "It is a nightmare to be fully responsible for business ownership – paying the rent, tax complexities, liability insurance, meeting payroll."
- "I would have to fully fund all marketing of the business and create customers from scratch."

After going through this exercise, in which we discover that many of us secretly dream of running our own business yet are faced with these obstacles, I offer the following proposition:

> *The profession of selling offers virtually all of the positive aspects of being an entrepreneurial business owner: managing your time; controlling your income based upon your own efforts and successes; being out in the business community rather than trapped in an office; and largely, being your own boss, as long as your performance meets expectations.*

The happy reality is that selling is the greatest business profession in the world. It gives such fantastic personal rewards, generally rewards offered only to business entrepreneurs, *without the personal risks* that are inherent in true business ownership.

What's more, the true beauty of the profession of selling is that it is purely an *achievement business*. In sales there is little concern for your personal background, social standing, race, gender, or where you went to school. Instead, all that matters is your performance! Aside from the world of professional sports, where your talent lets you rise to the top, I cannot think of another profession where performance matters so much to your standing in the organization.

The highly visible nature of the sales profession means it is not for the faint of heart. It is a job that attracts people who expect a lot of themselves and are willing to literally put their paycheck on the line every month. Salespeople make a bet with themselves each month that they are going to beat their performance standard in the interest of making a great living for their families. Many of the greatest rags-to-riches stories in business have their roots in salespeople who have created personal wealth and even fame from their extreme success in selling.

A successful salesperson acts both as a consultant for her customers and as a strategically-driven player advancing her organization's interests. It's a demanding task.

Being a Consultant *and* a Strategist

Providing added value today means understanding your customer's business, discovering how your organization can play a strategic role in the customer's business, and being able to communicate credibly with the customer's senior executives. It means understanding what influences customers' buying behaviors, anticipating those behaviors, and responding strategically. It requires you to understand how your customer uses your product or service over time and to establish profitable relationships between and within the buying and selling organizations. In short, you must be both a consultant *and* a strategist.

The roles of consultants and strategists are complementary, not opposed. They represent two sides of the same coin: sales effectiveness. The salesperson as consultant advances her customer's company by becoming a valued insider in the customer's business. The salesperson as a strategist advances her own company by outperforming the competition.

The Consultant

The salesperson acting in her consultant role gains an advantage by serving as a business consultant to her customers. By really understanding customers' risk and success factors, their products and processes, salespeople can position their offering in a way that links it to their *customer's* vision and strategy.

Customers face complexity in their businesses. The value a consultant can bring as an external resource may be to help customers make sense out of the issues they find themselves too close to to solve readily for themselves. Or they can bring expertise and information to customers that can improve the customers' business in innovative ways.

The Strategist

The salesperson acting in her role as strategist gains advantage for her organization by determining which business is most profitable to win, and then creating and implementing the appropriate competitive approach to winning that business.

So the strategic salesperson creates advantage in a sales campaign by developing a strategy that outsmarts, outperforms, and out-maneuvers the competition. As the sales campaign becomes more complex – requiring more contacts inside the organization and an increased ability to confront and overcome intensive competition – it is imperative that salespeople be equipped to develop an effective strategy.

Fred Perrotta entitled his signature book *Nothing Happens Until a Sale Is Made*. We could not agree more! Our job as a professional salesperson is important, exciting, lucrative, and generally very fulfilling. Sales has the blessed purity of being a profession that values nothing more than performance!

Keith Hawk

2 👎 Not Real: Faking Consultative Selling

A harsh reality of selling is that in far too many sales situations, we fail to make the customer more successful with our solutions. Rather, we simply attempt to convince him or her to buy our product rather than the competitors'. We become captivated by and focused only on our product's features, functions, and competitive price.

All too often, sales professionals merely profess to be on a problem-solving mission with a prospective customer. They begin by asking good questions about the customer's goals, objectives, and challenges. That's the right track, but then they make a fatal mistake that brands them as someone who is just trying to make a sale, not a true consultative professional.

That fatal mistake starts when a salesperson only listens for the first hint of a business problem that his or her product can impact. When the customer takes a breath as he explains his business challenges, the well-meaning salesperson breaks in with an "I can solve that" speech and begins pitching a product to the customer's problem. This premature delivery of a solution shuts down the customer's revelation of his critical success factors and business challenges and triggers his normal mode, *salesperson avoidance*.

People believe what *they say*, not what you say. By asking questions we help people uncover the difference between where they are today and where they could be. When that happens, our solutions are relevant – they make sense to the customer.

We must remember that none of our customers get up in the morning pondering *our* features, functions, or price. Rather, they get up wondering how they can improve *their* company's service. They agonize over how to make their business more profitable. They dream of getting home earlier from work to see a child's after-school activity – of gaining a higher quality of work and personal life.

If we simply recognize that it is OUR JOBS as sales professionals to relentlessly seek ways to *improve our customer's business* by discovering how to improve his company's ability to provide great service, profitability, and the quality of work life of his employees, we will be wildly successful. If we truly work this way, we will become that trusted advisor that our customers so sorely need. They will not commoditize our offering. They will not beat us up on price. They will not shop our solution around for the lowest bid. Rather, they will recognize that *we* are an added-value asset to their company because we are constantly seeking ways to make *them* more successful.

Thus our mantra: "My success can only follow the success of my customer!"

3 The True Purpose of a
Sales Professional – S.E.L.

A very wise mentor named George told me years ago that a Real sales professional has just three purposes. I have learned that if we hold true to these purposes we will gain intense clarity about what we do, how we do it, and how our customers view us.

Simply stated, as a consultative sales professional I am always seeking three things as I work to learn about the business of my customers. If I can discover these three things and structure my offerings based on one or more of them, my customer will be more successful as a result of my work. The principle that I hold as a sales professional is that *my success can only follow the success of my customer*. The acronym I use to remind myself of my selling purpose and methodology is S.E.L.

The *S* in S.E.L. stands for **Service** *to customers*. As a consultative sales professional I am continuously seeking ways to enhance my customer's capability to give exceptional service to *his* customers. If I discover ways in which my customer's business can serve *his* customer better, then I have tangible hooks on which to hang my product and service offerings. If I can help him make his company a better service provider, he will be more successful.

The *E* in S.E.L. stands for the **Economics** *of the firm*. As sales professionals, one of our most important roles is to seek ways to make our customer's business more profitable. There are really only two ways to make this happen:

1. Find ways to improve the *revenues* of the customer's firm. Demonstrate how your solution can help your customer find new opportunities for increasing his sales volume with *his customers*. Help him enter new markets. Add service capabilities to help your customer "up-sell" his current customers. Create new applications with the help of your products.
2. Find ways to reduce the *costs of operations* of the customer's business. Show how your product or service improves processes, reduces time of

production, requires less labor, etc.

In short, we must make it our business to find ways to positively impact the economics of our customer's business through our product and service solutions.

The *L* in S.E.L. stands for **Life**, specifically the quality of work life. Through our business solutions we should seek to find ways to enhance the quality of work life of the people who work in the customer's organization. Our solutions should make their lives easier, simpler, save them time, or spare them aggravation.

We promise our customers that we will never offer them products or services that do not positively support one or more of S.E.L.'s three key customer-impacting principles.

Keith Hawk

4 👎 Not Real: Selling Selfishly

Several clues tell you when a sales representative is selling to serve his or her own needs and interests, and not the customer's. Let's identify the signals of this self-serving focus from two perspectives: the sales process and the driving factors.

The "my needs" sales process starts with the mindset, "I need to make a sale today." You might say, "Well, of course she does, and what's wrong with that?" The answer is: *plenty!* When a salesperson starts with that mindset, it triggers a series of self-serving actions that place all the focus on her and her problem, and not the prospect's problem. She talks about:

- Who she is and how wonderful she is.
- What her product does and how great it is.
- How she has helped so many customers, thanks to what she sold them.

Also, as the "my needs" sales rep gets into the sales call, she asks very few questions – only enough to probe around what the prospect thinks he may need.

Then she immediately presents the product or service that will be easiest to sell, overwhelming the prospect with all its features and functionalities – and throughout this process she criticizes all his competitors' products and reputations.

All of that is just the warm-up for THE CLOSE. The "my needs" salesperson has armed herself with all the answers to every objection that the prospect could possibly think of. This is especially true about pricing challenges. If all else fails, the sales rep will discount as deeply as she thinks she needs to in order to get the deal, while protecting as much commission as possible for herself. She will ask, "What if I could offer you a one-time discount...?"

Once she gets the order, it becomes the home office's problem to deliver the product and satisfy the new customer. This salesperson will have already moved on to her next victim. Do you get the feeling we don't respect this approach?

5 Selling *On Purpose* – Is It Really an Art?

The true sales professional has a purpose and plan for every day. She knows where she's going, why she's going there, and what she will do when she arrives. What is really noticeable is how she is in control of herself and in command of the situation. This enables her to focus all her energies on the customer's interests, not her own.

She is selling *On Purpose!*

Let's observe a sales professional selling On Purpose, combining the science of selling with her own work of art. The initial conversation centers on the customer, not the seller. With unforced, high energy, the sales professional focuses on the contact's interests and situation. She quickly puts the contact at ease, explaining that the conversation will be about the contact's needs and interests, not her own. She purposefully establishes good intent by thoughtfully addressing questions she anticipates the contact may have. She says things like, "In preparing to meet you today, I thought you might have some questions, such as...." That's just the start.

What follows? Questions that lead to deeper discovery of the business, as well as competitive challenges that relate to the customer's situation and concerns. The purposeful sales professional knows that by getting the customer to talk openly, even confidentially, about current tasks, personal needs, and interests, she can discover the customer's core business issues. This helps her resolve business issues with solutions fashioned to provide benefits that address the Service-Economics-Life (S.E.L.) of the customer.

Just remember, the Purpose-driven sales professional:

- Focuses on the contact's needs, not her own.
- Puts the customer at ease, starting by addressing questions the customer may have.
- Asks thoughtful questions about the customer's situation and issues.
- Recommends solutions that benefit the contact's needs.
- Addresses all three elements of S.E.L.

As our business associate Steve Mulch says, "Sales is a science, artfully done!"

Are you selling On Purpose? If you are, you know it is one of the greatest of all sales differentiators. If you're not, you've got to give it a try!

6 👎 Not Real: The Easy Way

When I was growing up in Frog Hollow, Pennsylvania, I had three brothers to share life with, not to mention one bedroom and a single bathroom. Because we were a large family living in a small house, there were always chores to do.

My younger brother, J.D., often tried to find the easy way through his. Dad would admonish, "J.D., *when* are you going to learn that the hard way is the best way of getting the job done right?"

Now, that may not hold true for everything, but there is a golden nugget of wisdom in there. When I consult with senior executives today, I often hear, "Some of our salespeople are lazy." I ask myself why some people believe this. Our studies have identified five common characteristics of some salespeople that feed this troubling perception.

1. Salespeople are by nature more independent than other people in companies. They are perceived as not playing by the rules and being rebellious or poorly disciplined. They don't meet requirements that others meet, like working during defined hours, adhering to company policies, and following established processes.
2. Salespeople often oversell the capabilities of the company. Why? Because they think it's easier to just tell customers what they want to hear, rather than doing the hard work of discovering what customers truly need, and then matching those needs to a solution. Dad's point to J.D. was apt.
3. Others in the company often have to take care of the implementation needs of the customer because salespeople are conveniently not available for annoying meetings or present when "real work" actually gets done.
4. Salespeople get to do all the fun stuff, taking customers golfing and to business lunches. Their co-workers think they spend all the money and play much harder than they work.
5. Salespeople get all the glory, while the long-suffering people in the back office who do the unseen, unglamorous work get little or none. No won-

der those back office people – and others – think salespeople are over-paid for all the work they don't do! And no wonder there is sometimes friction between the salespeople and their support teams.

Sound familiar, possibly true? Get-Real sales professionals toe the line and don't support those stereotypes. So now let's explore some behaviors that are more favorable and productive.

Michael Boland

7 The Hard Way Is the Easy Way

Let's face it – in many ways, the world at large doesn't understand sales-people or their lives. However, before you start to throw a sales rep temper tantrum, yelling "Nobody understands me!" accept the fact that sometimes salespeople can be their own worst enemies. Ask: what can a salesperson do to earn understanding, support, and respect from his fellow salespeople, co-workers, management, and most of all, from his customers?

It starts with the fundamental tenets of Get-Real Selling. These attributes require dedication to your profession, which in the early stages can be hard to establish. These fundamentals will help you gain the respect of your managers and co-workers.

1. Play your role within your company team. Yes, selling is a team sport.
2. Recognize that your sales career plays a noble role in society. Sales is the greatest profession! Live the dream, every day!
3. Live and sell *On Purpose*. It's the cornerstone of being a contributing member of this profession, while delivering value to your customer, company, and community. It becomes your moral and professional compass.
4. Perform your role with an *outward* focus: first on your customer, and then on your company. Be consultative in all things, both as a problem solver and a strategist.
5. Be clear on what your goals are and what your plan for each day is, as well as your business objectives for this week, month, quarter, and year.
6. Work so that with every interaction with a customer, you are using at least one of the aspects of the S.E.L. model.
7. Be fit mentally, physically, emotionally, and spiritually by living a life of personal and professional balance.

When you work and live by these principles, your life is disciplined and responsible. You don't take short cuts in your job or your life. Yes, at times it may seem hard, and yet it is the best and most certain way to succeed. In the long run, the *hard way* really is the surest and *easiest way* to fulfillment.

8 Solutions Selling Defined – It Is Not a Fuzzy Concept!

Since IBM, XEROX, and AT&T brought us the sales process known as Systems Selling in the 1970s, many sales leaders have been consumed with the idea of having their sales professionals sell *solutions* – not *products*. This can be a difficult concept for sales managers and representatives to buy into and understand. In this chapter we will dramatically simplify how to go about becoming a *solutions-oriented* sales professional, abandoning the polar opposite – the *product-pushing, lead-with-discount-pricing* sales rep.

A good friend of ours named Rex is a sales VP in the Midwest leading a very large, highly successful team of sales professionals. Years ago he introduced us to the term *Bag Diver* to identify the salesperson who has little concern for what is going on in the customer's business as he goes about his sales job. The Bag Diver is only focused on himself and his company, seeing himself as a walking, talking product brochure that goes out into the business community reciting the features and advantages of his product, hoping that it resonates with some of the prospects he encounters. The Bag Diver requires little, if any, customer feedback – he is just seeking a "yes." Though the Bag Diver will run into situations where he will indeed make some sales, he gets orders more by dumb luck than by selling skill (see more on the evils of bag diving on page 32).

There is a much more efficient and effective way to sell – solutions selling. In our minds, it is based on three guiding principles:

1. My success as a salesperson can only follow the success of my customer.
2. As a salesperson, I am a business problem-solver. Rather than running headlong into a sales territory spouting off product features and price points, as a solutions-oriented sales professional I must first discover the most pressing business priorities of my customers. Then together we structure solutions that will help my customer successfully achieve these most important business imperatives.

3. I take the "S.E.L." approach (S = Service; E = Economics; L = Quality of Life). I constantly look for ways to improve my customer's Service offerings to *his customers*. Additionally, I seek ways to improve my customer's Economics (through helping him increase revenues and/or reduce expenses). Finally, I seek ways to improve the quality of work Life for the employees of my customer with my solutions.

Solutions selling is all about creating real sales opportunities by discovering ways to bring value to our customers through our company's solutions. We select business problems where we can make positive business impacts that are closely aligned to the interests of the customer decision-makers. Consistently employing this solutions approach, as opposed to always leading with product, is what sets apart the solutions seller from the typical Bag Diver.

9 👎 Not Real: Bag Diving as Your Method of Differentiation

As we've seen, Bag Divers are salespeople who simply make many sales calls each day, showing brochures and product features to anyone who agrees to see them. The approach is "Hey, stop me when you're ready to buy something" as they relentlessly talk about features, price, and the current sales promotion. A Bag Diver virtually dives into his bag of products, showering the prospect with brochures, and stresses the best price and feature combination in the market. You'll know you are dealing with a Bag Diver if you hear, "If you buy today I can get you a deal, since it's the end of the quarter."

The bag-diving pitchman simply lobs product purchase ideas across the desk at his prospect, hoping that something sticks and the prospective customer discovers a reason to do business together. Though this sounds grossly unprofessional, this approach is actually quite common and is in fact reinforced by the weekly sales quotas, product promotions, sales blitzes, and target lists that sales managers put in front of salespeople. Further, most sales training classes devote precious little time to discovering possible customer problems that can be solved with our solution. Instead, sales training often drives the bag-diving approach by focusing on feature comparisons with competitors, price points, the ordering process, and available options. Management's constant emphasis on units sold and weekly revenue generated, though necessary, reinforces bag-diving behavior.

Often when I speak on the problem-solving consultative approach to selling, I encounter skeptical salespeople who say, "Yeah, that sounds great, but it's not fast enough. I've got to move product NOW. I don't really have time to go discover and solve problems. I've got a weekly branch sales meeting in which I must tell my boss how many units I've sold and what's in my pipeline for next week."

This comment effectively says, "Though I would love to be genuinely successful, I don't have time for that. I would rather take what I think is the easy way and just run around the business landscape like a trained monkey, doing the same demo again and again, hoping I discover customers who are not looking at the competition and who already know what they need."

In our work with salespeople all over the world, we are frequently disappointed to find sales cultures that teach and reinforce bag-diving behaviors. This lack of focus on customer needs, driven by the *desire to make a sale now,* is what gives salespeople a bad name. The quality of the sales conversation is dramatically more important to one's ultimate selling success than the quantity of prospect meetings. We are convinced that selling is a noble *profession.* Salespeople who just run around their territory flashing brochures and offering promotional discounts are amateurs who need help!

10 Differentiation –
Live the Consultative Approach

Great sales professionals recognize that their job is to relentlessly understand and communicate what sets them and the solutions offered by their company apart from all others. We call this customer-focused, problem-solving approach Consultative Selling. We must constantly identify the important elements that set us apart from our competition *in the mind of our customer*. We cannot simply take a marketing-created message and inform our customer that we are distinctly different and better based upon documented product differences. Rather, we must make the effort to understand how our solutions can dramatically impact the performance of our customer's business and vividly demonstrate how our products and services will fulfill our customer's specific needs in ways that cannot be matched by our competition.

One of the biggest misperceptions salespeople make in their work is that it is their job to *show the product* to as many prospective customers as possible. This brute force approach assumes that if we just get out there we will find customers who are waiting to buy from us. It focuses solely on effort and is reinforced by sales managers chanting mantras like, *"Make one more call,"* or the old favorite, *"Let's have a selling BLITZ!"* You see it in many books on selling too. These high-effort, low-engagement approaches can yield some results, but they do not win long-term business, nor do they position the sales professional as a value-added resource to his or her customers.

True sales professionals realize that they must *differentiate* to truly reach selling success and to establish long-term business relationships with their customer base. In his classic article, "Marketing Success through Differentiation," Theodore Levitt writes, "There is no such thing as a commodity. All goods and services are differentiable." Differentiation is possible on virtually every level. The thinking sales professional can differentiate on service, product, company commitment, relationship, problem-solving approach, pricing creativity, and many other elements.

The most difficult challenge for sales professionals is to avoid the temptation to presume that the best claim for differentiation comes from providing the lowest price. Having the lowest price in the market is not a sustainable advantage. It can be trumped at any time by a determined competitor. Though all customers want the feeling that they are getting a great deal, they do not buy just because of the deal. They buy because they are seeking to fix a problem in their business, to start a new revenue opportunity, or to make a business process easier. Though price competition is an interesting way to get their attention, it will not make them buy. After the purchase decision is made, price becomes a distant memory. What the customer does remember is the effectiveness with which our solution helps him achieve his objective. If we consistently help our customers to succeed, we will become trusted advisors who have a degree of insulation from having to provide the lowest price in order to win the business.

11 Differentiation in the Real World

It is not always necessary to invent totally new products in order for a company to differentiate itself from the competition. In fact, some of the greatest examples of differentiation are based upon companies that found that providing better service experiences for their customers was the most direct route to differentiation. Following are real-life examples of how businesses set themselves apart and achieved great riches by being willing to depart from the norm and focus on what customers really wanted. These examples feature a particular focus on *the WAY customers want to get and use the products* as their principle point of differentiation. Read on and consider how you can tailor your offering to your customers' preferences for buying and using *your* products and services!

Avis – In the 1970s when confronted by the problem of being "Number Two" in the car rental industry, Avis found ways to differentiate from market leader Hertz, as well as all those lower cost providers that were nipping at their market share from below. Avis actually studied their customer base, listening to their woes about *the process of renting a car*. They found that they could differentiate on this process, rather than taking the traditional approach of differentiating on the product (the car) itself. They invented Avis Preferred, eliminating the frustration of waiting in long lines, filling out endless paperwork, answering questions about insurance, and picking up the keys at a busy airport desk. By *simplifying the process of renting and picking up the vehicle* and marketing this advantage with the "We try harder" tagline, Avis was able to differentiate itself from the competition in meaningful ways, recognizing that the process of acquiring and using the product could be as important as the product itself to the consumer. Note that it is necessary to *continue* to differentiate, as every meaningful competitor then followed the Avis Preferred customer program with one of their own.

Starbucks – People had been buying coffee in retail establishments for centuries before Starbucks was born. Starbucks seized on the idea that they could multiply the value/price ratio of a cup of coffee by creating a soothing, hip, trendy environment and extending the product line with special mixes and flavors that went beyond what the traditional coffee shop provided. They continue to differentiate and extend the product line with such leading innovations as wi-fi connections in the shops, low fat-pastries, and even Starbucks-branded breath mints. Starbucks focused on *the experience* of buying and consuming the coffee rather than just the product itself as their way to dramatically differentiate themselves and build one of the most powerful consumer brands in the world.

Arena Football League – Commissioner David Baker recognized through the success of the National Football League that Americans could not get enough football. He launched a fledgling indoor, off-season league to serve up an exciting brand of football that is played inside basketball and hockey arenas. How did he differentiate the new sport? He designed it to avoid things that irritate regular football fans - punting, low scores, boring halftimes, overpaid players, and expensive tickets. Baker structured the rules to maximize offensive play, keep the action almost constant, and eliminate virtually all of the irritants. His league has soared in popularity and now it is a viable off-season form of football entertainment. He also appealed to a broader fan base by making it a much more affordable option than the much higher-priced NFL game tickets.

Domino's Pizza – In the early days of its existence, Domino's Pizza found themselves in a pizza delivery marketplace that was crowded with competitors. Through surveying their target markets Domino's Pizza learned what was most important to their customers: fast, free delivery. Though they still emphasized the quality of their pizza and they made extensive use of couponing, Domino's Pizza's core differentiation technique was built around delivery. To imprint their value proposition with their market targets, they aggressively advertised on TV, radio, and in print, using their tagline, "30 Minutes or Free." They stressed the differentiable point that, when buying from Domino's Pizza, you won't suffer from delayed gratification - your pizza will arrive soon after you order.

K9-KLEEN – One of our favorite examples of a business discovering what the market really wants is this small but growing firm based on a very simple concept. They recognized that people like to wash their own dogs but do not have a convenient place to do so at home. K9-KLEEN provides tubs made for just this purpose – plus dog shampoo, dryers, and other doggie supplies for customers to come in and use – at half the price of going to a full-fledged "dog groomer." Interestingly, what they sell can be done at home at a fraction of the cost, yet they are booming because they have created a pleasant way to get through what was a messy task.

Dell – Just a few years ago an entrepreneurial young man named Michael Dell seized upon the idea of providing mail and Internet-order computers that were custom made. Though his computers are not necessarily the top of the line in terms of quality or performance, he has built a pristine brand and a super-power business based on flexibility and speed of delivery. He discovered that computer buyers love the idea of being able to go online and build their own computer by selecting options. Dell also knew that he could hold costs down by minimizing the need for stocking finished inventory and for distribution in retail outlets. His principle point of differentiation is personal choice – giving each buyer a chance to create a custom-made computer.

You'll note that these examples focus on companies, not individuals. Your job as a Real sales professional is to seek ways to differentiate yourself as a salesperson. You cannot afford to wait for your company to do all the differentiation for you. Your consultative, business problem-solving approach is the place to start your *personal differentiation* campaign. Here are some examples of how you can differentiate yourself in the minds of your customers:

- Create training seminars within your customer's organization that assure that the benefits your decision-maker valued when he bought from you are implemented throughout the organization.
- Create spreadsheet details of the "total value of ownership" of your solution, based on S.E.L., so that the customer cannot just focus on the price of your product. Show how you improve your customer's Service to his customers; how you improve his Economics by helping his company make more money or save on expenses; detail the quality of Life benefits that will occur for his employees.
- Brief your installation team on each sale you have made. Help them make the installation unique, even personal. Make sure your implementation team has an in-depth understanding of *why the customer bought from us,* so they can reinforce those great reasons when they deliver and install the solution for the users.

12 Half of Winning Is Just Showing Up

There is no substitute for human contact in business-to-business selling.

As much as each of us have days when we would love some delightful magic that would make people buy our products and services without our having to interact with them, there is no substitute for talking with your customer. Said another way, we must get out there and sell, whether in person or by phone.

If I am in the Internet retail business I may be able to achieve sales just by appealing to people who are window shopping online. However, if I am a business-to-business professional selling problem-solving solutions, I must remember that people do not typically become interested in my product offerings until they discover that they have a need (usually with my help), and they will require that I personally advocate my solution, handle their objections, negotiate terms, and plan for implementation.

Despite our admonishments to get out there with your customers, we do understand the very real need to aggressively fill the sales pipeline with opportunities. There *are* some ways to make things happen more quickly than just the arduous process of seeing your customers one-by-one, in person. We have significant first-hand experience with the need to identify and develop opportunities efficiently and quickly. Here are some thoughts on moving rapidly into a sales territory without reverting to the NOT REAL ideas we've pointed out previously:

Don't kid yourself: *Target Identification* is one of your most important jobs as a sales professional. Do not waste your time on *suspected* buyers or users of your solution. Work very hard to focus on people who are truly *prospective* buyers. Make sure that you clearly identify the type of individual who will be the buyer of your solution. Most of your efforts should be targeted to their specific needs and characteristics. (Too often we settle for calling on "whoever will see me" within a customer account).

Work hard to establish the way in. Assuming you are working within an established business that has a track record of selling success, there are identifiable methods, practices, and tactics that those who came before you have used. Carefully study the selling processes that your firm's most successful sales professionals use. For example, do not assume that prospective customers are just awaiting your call so they can sit in fascination as you describe the features and functions of your widget. Rather, assume that your target customer is surrounded by problems that need solutions. As we have said repeatedly, your job is to make your customer's business operate more effectively. Your approach should be totally built around solving the problems they are having accomplishing their business objectives.

Part 2

Tried and True: Get-Real Sales Skills, Processes, and Tactics That Will Transform You into a True Consultative Sales Professional

"No matter if you're just getting started in sales or you're a seasoned pro, it's essential that you are *consciously in control* of every aspect of your selling."

This section dives deeper into specific selling tactics and skills so you can hone them. You will learn about account management, who to call on, and how to adapt to your customer's buying preferences. You'll also consider a Get-Real definition of being *strategic* in your selling efforts. Finally, you'll hear our views on the much-debated topic of Closing.

13 👎 Not Real: The Big-Hitter Approach: Part One of a Fable

This is a story that is played out every day in the sales world. In Shakespeare's time it would have been called a tragedy, a story that is sad but true.

Judy is a newly hired sales rep assigned to a territory that had been poorly covered by John, the previous rep who was terminated two months earlier. Thanks to his poor performance and the recent gap in coverage, the customer base has been picked apart by the competition and the territory is in a general state of decay. Judy, who has limited sales experience, is relying on her manager, Tom, to provide her with the training on the product knowledge and selling skills that she needs to succeed.

As often happens, Judy receives adequate product training, but her sales skills training is basically "on the job." It consists of Tom showing her the standard sales approach that his current "big hitters" use. These heroes are actually a couple of fast-talking, high-bravado sales representatives who talk big at weekly sales meetings, and usually in sound bytes. Their approach is purely "my needs" based, meaning they mostly focus on *their need* to make sales, especially at the end of each month and quarter. They boast of being hard closers and cultivating great personal relationships that have customers eating out of their hands.

In the early stages, Judy's attempt to merge Tom's sales training with her own intuitive sales approach does not succeed. After three months of marginal progress, Tom puts Judy on a "performance plan." Judy is discouraged and feels that the company and her manager are setting her up to fail. The performance plan is simply Tom's way of telling her to go find a new job. In the end, everyone loses: Judy, Tom, their company, the customers. Everyone, that is, except the competition.

14 When in Doubt, Go Study Your Customer's Business! Part Two of a Fable

Judy is stunned by Tom's move to put her on a performance plan. Figuring she has nothing to lose, she decides to sell in her own style. She instinctively knows that there is a better way to approach her prospects and existing customers, one that could serve all parties' interests – the customer's, her company's, and her own - much more effectively. She decides that if she is going to make it in sales, it must be on terms she can live with.

Judy commits to a more customer-focused sales process, one that takes a problem-solving approach for developing new business and growing existing accounts.

She starts by putting herself in the shoes of the prospects, and realizing they have questions and concerns about:

- Judy and her company
- Why she is really there
- What she knows about them and their challenges
- What Judy can actually do for them
- Whether she will be there when they have a problem in the future (see our Pre-Call Planner in the Appendix)

Judy develops her approach to address each one of those questions.

Her contacts seem to respond well. They feel that Judy is genuinely interested in their success, and they trust that she is there for their best interests as well as her own. They see that she puts their needs before her own. Judy sticks to this consultative approach, and by the end of her first year her performance is more productive, consistent, and dependable than her big-talking counterparts on the sales team.

Becoming a consultative salesperson feels a bit like a conversion experience. You must have the courage and commitment to take the plunge. For salespeople, it can be a difficult choice. They find it hard to let go of the sales habits and beliefs that give them their current results (which are often just average or mediocre). However, once they learn and practice these problem-solving skills as they sell, they see positive results. Customers become more trusting, enabling the sales professional to collaborate with them on their problems and opportunities. The successes of Real sales professionals always follow from the success of the customer.

Being consultative actually becomes a way of life. You approach all the challenges and opportunities you encounter more effectively and efficiently. Others, including your spouse, children, and friends, start looking to you to provide leadership and guidance. You may become an unofficial leader, known for solving problems and creating new solutions in your home, place of worship, service organization, and community. It becomes a part of *who you are*. Becoming a person who sees his or her primary role as helping others become more successful is a noble role. It also gives you a great feeling of accomplishment and fulfillment!

15 Business Acumen as Your Personal Differentiator

One of the strongest differentiators of the Real sales professional is his grasp of what is truly important to his customer. In addition to using the S.E.L. approach, another critical skill of professionals is their in-depth understanding of business principles. Consciously competent sales professionals consistently do three things to develop their business acumen in a way that supports sales efforts.

First, business acumen starts with research, which makes you knowledgeable about the customer's business and industry. Customers today no longer have the time or inclination to thoroughly educate sales people about their business. You simply must do your homework before you make a sales call. It requires ability and discipline to secure and analyze data, including financial reports, but the payoffs are big. When you can paint a picture of the customer's business based upon key indicators that you monitor about his business, you can begin to draw conclusions about your customer's competitive performance and overall financial health. This knowledge will help you work more quickly in identifying opportunities.

Second, it is essential that you conduct your own person-to-person "discovery" to confirm or correct your analysis of the company you are identifying as a potential sales opportunity. This on-the-ground questioning will lead you to the opportunities that will help you improve your S.E.L. by improving your customer's *service* to his clientele, his *economics*, and the quality of *life* of his employees. You are very likely to develop opportunities for improvement that your customer has not yet identified. Consistently proving your worth in this way becomes your personal differentiator against your competition.

The third important element is to continually work to connect with high performers across various functions in the customer's organization. They know what it takes for their business to be successful. To achieve these connections across the customer organization requires you to develop the versatility to sustain professional relationships with a wide variety of personalities.

Boost Your Business Acumen

Deepening your knowledge of how businesses operate requires some dedication to continuous personal development and learning. If you devote 20 minutes per day to growing your understanding of the world of business, you'll soon see big gains. The following are several suggested online sources of daily reading that will expand your business acumen:

CNN Money: money.cnn.com – Financially-oriented business news
Forbes: Forbes.com – Business news and analysis
Freerealtime.com – Business information focused on the stock market
LexisNexis: Lexisnexis.com – Business and legal news and information
TheStreet.com – The stock markets
Wall Street Journal online edition: wsj.com – Domestic and international business news and analysis
Financial Times: ft.com – Business news
Any trade journals, newspapers, or websites with news from the business sectors your customers work in – check on Google or other search engines

16 Searching for New Selling Opportunities

Wise old sales managers often say, "The best source of new opportunities is within your existing accounts." Much has been written about the time, expense, and overall difficulty of opening new accounts. In new accounts we typically start small by establishing some sort of beachhead, surrounded by competing products that have tenure and a track record. On the other hand, with existing customers we are a known supplier with proven capabilities. It just stands to reason that we should think "expand and up-sell" at least as much as we think about new account development as we search for new selling opportunities in our territory.

Have you ever said to yourself, "I have already sold that account" when looking at a list of current customers? That's Not Real thinking. We must make a habit of continuously expanding our "wallet share" within our current accounts. Putting it another way, if one department or one floor of a big company buys from me I will not consider that I have maximized my opportunities in that account until I have implanted my solutions in every department and/or on every floor, assuming I can continue to find ways to enhance my customer's business by adding my solutions within their operation.

This practice drove Xerox to great heights in the 1970's. In the early days of photo copiers, a company bought one copier to cover the needs of huge populations of business users. Xerox learned to keep spreading the applications for their products to smaller and smaller subsets of their existing customers. They were so successful that in addition to the original "copy centers" that existed in companies, their customers started buying copiers for individual departments and, in some cases, for individual users.

So, Job One in seeking new opportunities is to assure that you are maximizing your sales potential within your existing customers. Beyond that it is generally considered very healthy sales behavior to always have a pipeline of new business opportunities that you are working on to keep your territory green and growing. That's because inevitably, negative events (e.g., business closings, company consolidations, and occasional competitive losses), will take their toll, so it is vital that you always have a stream of new revenues from new accounts in your territory. Over time these new accounts will be the foundations of your business as you up-sell them.

Where do we find opportunities? That depends on the type of business you are in. Some companies will provide reps with leads generated from marketing efforts. In others, salespeople are expected to find or make their own opportunities. As a sales professional I consider the rise of the Internet to be the greatest tool yet for gathering background information on prospects. I can purchase data downloads of companies in a target SIC code. I can go to a company website to learn who decision-makers are. I can setup automatic alerts on LexisNexis that inform me when news is breaking about my prospects. There are numerous applications that give me instant access to information that, in pre-Internet times, were just too difficult to get. My job now becomes developing my abilities to target opportunities with precision, not just search for companies. Yes, it is a great era in which to be a sales professional!

17 👎 Not Real: Sales as a Remote-Control Business

We hate to see salespeople wasting time, sitting at a desk and "putting things out there" to drive sales back to them, rather than getting out there (either by phone or in person) to develop opportunities. Here are several wrong-way examples we have witnessed first-hand:

1. The Magic Letter: We chuckle when we see sales reps writing the perfect prospect letter to create interest in what they sell. They crow, "If I can mail out 5,000 letters and generate a 5 percent response, I will have 250 qualified leads to work on!" Consider that 4,750 of the letters will be treated as junk mail and trashed immediately. Just ask yourself, "Would I respond myself to this letter?"
2. The Magic E-mail: The same flawed thinking, updated. Like the Magic Letter approach, you risk getting snagged by your prospect's spam catcher – not a good start for your relationship. It's hard to distinguish your best-intentioned notes from obvious spam.
3. Selling via Voicemail: Recently a wildly enthusiastic salesperson introduced himself to my voicemail and then left a long message about the virtues of his product. I had never spoken with him. He knew nothing about my business or its issues. This was literally a random sales pitch. He closed, saying, "I will await your call." I'm sure my pathetic caller was being pressed by his sales manager to get more opportunities into his pipeline. I wonder what chance of success he gave his "opportunity" with me when he put me into his next sales forecast!

Bottom Line: Do not waste your time on things that delude you or your management into thinking you are creating opportunities by remote control! Focus on the end result and be as accountable to yourself as you are to your company leadership.

Keith Hawk

18 Effective Techniques for Reducing Relationship Tension

The first moments of initial meetings are filled with what we call *relationship tension*. That's the natural tendency to be a bit reserved until you get to know someone and feel a degree of trust. So what do sales professionals do to overcome relationship tension and get down to the business of solving customers' business problems? We offer two very specific techniques aimed at establishing trust, enhancing your credibility as a sales professional, and framing the purpose of the business meeting.

1. Make sure your customer quickly learns *who you are, how you work, and what your company's core purpose is.* Very shortly after the initial handshake with a new customer or contact, a consciously competent sales professional moves to answer the following questions, knowing they are on the new person's mind:

   - "Who are you and what have you done?" It is vital that you introduce your past experience, professional certifications, and one or two examples showing how you have solved serious customer business problems.
   - "What does your company stand for?" You must also give a concise overview in clear business terms of what your company does to improve the customer's ability to serve his own customers, improve his economics, and the upgrade the quality of work life for himself or his organization (yes, that's S.E.L. again!). This cannot be a list of fuzzy platitudes. It needs to be razor sharp, meaningful, and memorable. For example: "My firm is in the business of providing solutions to help companies like yours reduce their accounts receivable. Our solutions always pay for themselves – we guarantee it."
   - "How do you work?" Your answer recaps the S.E.L. approach. Here's one formulation: "Our methodology is to interview key department

leaders within your organization to understand your current business processes. Then, where possible, we bring you business solutions that improve your service to your customers, enhance your economics (through either increased revenues or reduced expenses), and improve the quality of work life for you and your employees through our efficiency-driving business solutions."

2. Establish *precisely* why we are meeting today, how we will work when we are together, and what could the customer possibly gain by meeting with you. There is no substitute for eliminating uncertainty in a business relationship. People want to have a sense of where they are going and how they will get there. *Give them this certainty* within the first five minutes of every one of your business meetings. It will allow you to focus much more quickly on the task at hand and make your customer or prospect feel more at ease. It also builds your credibility and whets his appetite for what is possible. Be an absolutely open book with your customer about your intentions and about how you will work together. Remind him or her that "My success can only follow your success!"

Effectively using these techniques puts the contact at ease and enables you to redirect relationship tension to the task at hand, focusing on the customer's business challenge and opportunities.

19 👎 Not Real: Being Defeated by the Fear of Calling High

For many salespeople, there is nothing more challenging or frightening than having to make a critical sales call on an executive high up in an important account's organization. This anxiety causes them to think such thoughts as:

- "What if the executive says no when I ask for the appointment?"
- "What does this executive know that I don't know?"
- "He has the power to make me or break me on this deal."
- "I know she has a favorite supplier and we're not it."
- "If I blow this call with him I will lose the account forever."

Once a salesperson gives these self-defeating thoughts and fears credence, he may do one of three things. Each of them can prevent him from achieving his objective of successfully calling on the executive.

1. The sales rep may use a gimmick to get the executive's attention.
2. He may attempt to make the contact without thinking through the process. If he's lucky, he gets the executive's voicemail and leaves a brief, meaningless message, which is sure to get no response. Worse still, he actually connects with the executive, and then stammers and stutters through a disastrous call that wastes the executive's time.
3. He may just put the call off, hoping his relationship with his lower level contacts will be sufficient to sell within the account.

The more sophisticated you are about the political structure of customer organizations, the more you understand how critical it is to gain access to senior leaders. They may not be our normal day-to-day contacts, yet we need to see them from time to time to solve problems, move obstacles, gain perspective, or get a decision. So don't defeat yourself by letting fears keep you from contacting executives, and be prepared when you get through.

20 "Why Are You Calling on this Person?" "Because He'll See Me!"

A critical aspect in achieving sales professional mastery is whom you call on in your territory. You must know for certain who the influencers and buyers of your business solutions are. Amazingly, many salespeople are not particularly "targeted" about whom they call on. Thus the title for this chapter – an old joke among sales managers.

Though the concept of calling on the right people within your customer base seems simple and logical, the reality is that often we find it challenging to get these people to see us. (Probably because they are busy making important decisions and working with the other key players in their organization, or else seeing your competitor.) So we often call on lesser players in an organization, people who enjoy taking our appointments. While these peripheral players may share useful knowledge about the organization and its priorities, they will not take us all the way to the sale. For that, we must deal with decision-makers and people who influence those decisions.

There many books on the topic of "calling high," or getting to owners. In *Setting Sales Appointments: How to Gain Access to Top Level Decision-Makers*, Scott Channel correctly says, "Meeting more of the right people face-to-face in quantity will improve your closing ratio and bank balance remarkably." As consciously competent sales professionals who want to be efficient and productive, we intuitively know that we should be spending most of our customer "face time" with the key people in the customer's organization who will lead us most directly to the sale. Anthony Parinello, in his sales classic, *Selling to VITO (Very Important Top Officer)*, adds that "VITOs are the people with the ultimate veto power who hold the key to bigger commission checks, every sales award you could possibly win, and referrals that you can take to the bank."

Let's examine the specific reasons why it is important that we meet with the leaders within our customer organizations:

- Leaders make buying decisions. There are very few decision makers in an organization when it comes down to spending significant sums of money. Leaders will not make a buying decision without understanding the risks and rewards of the decision and the ultimate benefits that will be gained by making a significant purchase.
- Leaders make the budgets. Businesses have revenue and expense budgets. In order for a company to buy your product or service they must "find the money" to invest in your solution from a budget. In virtually every company, business leaders have fiscal policies that guide them to assure they are "in balance" with their revenues and expenses, with their ultimate measure being profitability.
- Leaders can move budget money around. This critical fact is ignored by many salespeople. We often hear the objection, "I'm sorry. I really would like to buy your solution, but I just do not have it in my budget. Maybe next year." This response is a sure sign that you are not dealing with a true business leader. If your product can make a meaningful impact on your customer's business, (e.g., increase revenues, reduce overall expenses, improve service to their customers in meaningful ways), a true business leader will re-prioritize company spending and find money for your solution by de-prioritizing other spending plans that will have less impact. If you always had to wait for budgeting, you would never sell anything of substance.
- Leaders' insights will lead you to new opportunities. People who run the company speak in broad terms about the major priorities of the organization. They wrestle with the obstacles to achieving those priorities. You will learn things that can impact your selling plans significantly by listening carefully to their most pressing problems. Hopefully, you will find ways to assist them in achieving their aims by employing your products and services.
- Leader connections give you a definite competitive advantage. Most sales professionals work at levels that are too low for effective influence in their accounts. If you can find ways to develop relationships with people who call the shots, it will help you overcome the lesser differentiation points (e.g., price, features) as well as the minor advantages that your competition will stress in their attempts to defeat you. Seek referrals *within the organization* from the leaders you speak with. Their endorsement with

their peers will allow you to rise above the other competition.

Leaders are more fun to work with! They think big thoughts and make big plans. They work with other senior leaders in the community. They are generally very smart people who see business as a dynamic challenge. Business is not just a job to them – it is an important mission. You will be more invigorated by the challenge of working with leaders who are solving business problems and reaching for big gains than by working down at the implementer level where the pricing, delivery, and product features are constant refrains.

21 The Importance of Establishing Trust and Credibility

We have used the S.E.L. concept as the platform around which we build our value proposition to our customers for years. It is important to ask, "Why will our customers even listen to us in the first place? What gives us a chance to go do our good work that leads to effective S.E.L. solutions?"

We have our friends at Wilson Learning Corporation to thank for some very effective skills and techniques that are taught in their signature program, *The Counselor Sales Process*. Here are a few key techniques that have proven time and again to help us win the trust and respect of our customers as we work to solve their business problems with our solutions.

How do we overcome the initial obstacle of lack of familiarity or even a lack of trust in us in our customer?

Technique #1: Ben Duffy. Though you will need to take the Consultative Sales Process course to get a full understanding and to practice it yourself, in short, this technique immediately puts customers at ease with the knowledge that you have *their* best interests at heart. Use this technique very early in the initial meeting with a customer. *You must anticipate and answer questions the customer will have about you, your company, and how you do business.* You share your anticipated questions and answers with the customer as a way to get started. This empathetic approach demonstrates that you really can and do think as the customer does, including addressing tough questions that you must overcome before you can move forward. The technique builds credibility and trust very quickly. As opposed to traditional hard charging, early closing, product pushing, brochure flipping sales methods, the Ben Duffy technique will relax your customer with the knowledge that you are there to serve and that you are worth working with!

Technique # 2: Purpose – Process – Payoff. Wilson Learning also pioneered this elegantly simple way to demonstrate preparation, thoughtfulness, and an organized mind at the start of a meeting, phone call or written communication. Simply stated, you begin the event by sharing the *very specific reason for it* (PURPOSE). Then you describe *how we will work when we are together or how the call or document will be structured* (PROCESS). Finally, you describe *how the customer can benefit from this event* (PAYOFF). Here is an example:

"Ms. Jones, I am here today to help discover ways that we might be able to help your organization reduce your days-sales-outstanding totals from their relatively high level presently to a more industry-standard time period (Purpose). The way that we can accomplish this discovery will involve about a 20-minute conversation with you, followed by individual meetings that I will have with your CFO and your Accounts Receivable personnel to learn the details of your current process. Within two days, I will of course share all my findings with you in what I call a Discovery Agreement (Process). It is likely that you will reap the same improvements in your collections time frame that many of my other customers are already enjoying (Payoff). How does that sound?"

With Purpose-Process-Payoff statements, we continue to build on that wave of trust and credibility that we set out to establish from the beginning with our core concept – that *we can only be successful as a company when we make our customers more successful.*

Practice and consistent use of these techniques will ensure that you are gaining trust and credibility so you can proceed to discover how you can help your customer be more successful. She will only help you get to this point after she trusts you and recognizes that you have the skills, knowledge, and positive intentions to put her interests ahead of your own. This approach provides a direct pathway to the S.E.L. philosophy: "Our success can only follow the success of our customer."

22 👎 Not Real: Being Out of Sync with Customers' Buying Interests

Few things are more frustrating to sales reps than dealing with prospects or customers who just can't see, or refuse to accept, all the value that a salesperson provides along the way while selling his product or service. This situation becomes even more irritating when the sales rep feels that he has followed a sales process that included a good discovery and analysis of what the customer's needs are. There are actually two extremes in which we find salespeople caught up in this peculiar dilemma.

Prospects and customers tend to operate at some point on a continuum that illustrates their preferred level of involvement with a sales representative. At one extreme, they tend to keep the sales rep at arms' length, by having either rules that prevent salespeople from getting too close to the buyer(s), or by behaving in a way that indicates that all they want is a vendor to provide a basic offering and no more.

The other extreme is the situation in which the prospect wants to have a closer working relationship, one which will require a lot of time and energy, and yet provides no guarantee that the rep will get the business after putting all that effort into it.

Sales reps tend to gravitate toward one extreme or the other as well. We all know sales reps who believe they can rely on personal, rather than business, relationships to achieve their sales objectives with various customers. This can cause salespeople to get bogged down, devoting a lot of time and resources to each customer, which constrains their ability to serve all the customers and prospects in their territory or account base.

At the other extreme are the sales reps that like to do drive-by selling ("I just stopped by to see if you need anything today"), with very low commitment of time or resources to each customer. This tends to inhibit the growth of trusting relationships with customers. These reps usually rely on product features, functionality, price, and delivery to win the business.

The challenge is for the sales rep to *match the prospect or customer's prefer-*

ence with their sales approach. Naively assuming that customers wish to buy the same way you want to sell is counter-productive. We must remember that *we* are serving *their* needs – not the other way around.

23 Reading and Adapting to the Customer's Buying Preference

Thoughtfully led sales organizations sometimes segment their markets by the ways various customers prefer to buy what they sell. This segmentation is often divided into three categories, ranged along a continuum. On one end are customers who prefer a total solution and are willing to pay for it. In the middle ground customers prefer some of the amenities that accompany the solution, and they value them. On the other extreme, customers want only the basic product or service, at the lowest possible price. Think of the business class traveler; the coach class traveler; and the last-minute, no-frills, I-don't-care-where-I-go-as-long-as-it's-warm traveler.

Organizations and salespeople recognize that there are costs associated with each of these segments, including the investment of their time. Misjudging what the customer prefers can be costly in a variety of ways, from being perceived as not competitive to over-investing your greatest resource, time. This assessment process resembles the tale of the three bears looking for the chair, porridge, and bed that were each "juuuuuust right."

Flexible sales professionals have a keen sense for the degree of interaction that a given customer prefers. It starts with understanding the customer's point of view, commonly referred to as the customer's buying behavior.

Our friends from Wilson Learning use a tool based upon the work of Barbara Bund, called the *Account Behavior Spectrum*. It identifies the customer's buying traits and charts them on a continuum that describes customer preferences, ranging from highly interactive, Relational styles to minimally interactive, Transactional ones. These preferences are typically driven by the customer's own business conditions, culture, and requirements.

There is no good or bad, right or wrong place to be on this continuum. What matters is that the sales professional understand the customer's preferred method for buying what he is offering, and then align his sales strategies and value proposition with the customer's interests. Sales professionals can be successful with all types of buyers, and many actually prefer to have a portfolio of accounts located all across that spectrum.

Being tightly aligned with the customer's buying preferences can pay big dividends. For customers who are relational, sales professionals create more effective value-added, strategic sales approaches. For purely transactional customers, they develop no-frills, "WYSIWYG" (What You See Is What You Get) solutions that are based upon price, terms, function, and delivery.

Finally, being sensitive to what level of interaction the customer prefers enables you to provide just the right level of sales effort, from product vendor to problem solver to trusted advisor, or even a business partner.

All of this is designed to *meet the customer where they are* on the spectrum. This optimizes the return on the resources your organization invests, and it also reduces tension in the sales process. Being aware of buyers' preferences enables Real sales professionals and their companies to win more business and to secure sustainable competitive advantage.

24 Discovery: The Most Direct Path to Sales Success

Of all the steps of the sales process, save for closing, nothing is talked about more and done less than the gathering of useful information on our customer's business drivers and obstacles to success. In Chapter 2 we described sales reps that try to fake being consultative, by asking just enough questions to get a hint of the customer's need, so they can begin bag diving – pitching their product.

We are convinced that this step of the sales process, called Discovery, is the cornerstone of the consultative sales process. It is the phase where the consummate sales professional must be most consciously competent. Discovery is the one skill area where practice will be richly rewarded. Why is this so critical? Let's explore the reasons why discovery is important then describe the key elements of this vital process.

Why is discovery important? There is nothing quite so valuable to a sales professional as spending time listening to his customer describe his business opportunities and challenges. Our job in this conversation is not to talk. Rather, our job is to listen, restate for understanding, and seek the implications of these business interests. We are seeking a vividly clear understanding of our customer's business situation so that we may ultimately deliver ways to help him maximize his success. The fundamental role of a consultant is to discover, i.e., to reveal and diagnose, what the customer's root issues are regarding his business situation. Doing detailed discovery broadens and adds colorful detail to those needs, which transforms our ultimate recommendation from being product focused to being solutions oriented.

Elements of the discovery process:

1. Develop your discovery strategy before you meet. Do your homework, list what you need to find out and how you'll find it, map out how you'd like the meeting to flow.
2. Ask questions that get at both the facts and the emotions involved in

the situation. Probe more deeply once the initial facts and emotions have been stated so that you have an accurate, detailed picture of the situation.

3. Be nimble. You must be able to go where the questions lead you. Get to the root problems and their causes.

4. Pursue both "task motives" and "personal motives" relentlessly (see Chapter 37. The sales professional who can uncover these, especially the personal motives of influencers and decision-makers, will gain competitive advantage.

5. Be an attentive listener. Clear your mind and silence your inner voice. Take notes. Ask clarifying questions. Probe for understanding. Your job is to find your customer's most daunting challenges so that you can create solutions that truly impact his or her business.

6. Based on what you learn, identify a vividly clear gap between the customer's current state and what the desired state looks like. Identify the barriers that are creating that gap. Determine what the total costs of this gap are to the customer. This gap will enable you to position your solution in sync with your customer's needs.

7. Playing back the critical data you learn via discovery assures your customer that you have heard him clearly and captured his information accurately – something that rarely happens in business. This enables you to create a compelling solution that the customer is prepared to accept. If you become proficient at discovery it will become your greatest personal differentiator.

We are absolutely convinced of this: *Discovery is the sales professional's greatest source of competitive advantage, and the one least utilized.*

Why is this skill the least developed one for the majority of salespeople in the world? There are three basic reasons:

1. Reluctance to learn and practice discovery skills.

2. Choosing what some perceive is the easier path of being a Bag Diver rather than a consultative sales professional.

3. Letting ego get in the way. Ego drives us to talk. Consultative selling and discovery are all about asking questions and listening.

In our combined sixty-plus years of sales and management experience, we have found nothing more critical to sales success than mastering discovery skills. As we study great sales professionals around the world, we learn that the one characteristic they all share is an absolute commitment to finding out what makes their customers tick. They do this every day, using *Discovery*.

25 The Magic Question

It is essential that you first see yourself in a different way in order to become a Real, solution-oriented sales professional. *You must see yourself as a person whose job is to make business operate more efficiently and effectively for your customers.* You do this by seeking to understand their business operation more accurately than before. Surprisingly, this is not necessarily difficult or time consuming. We have one simple question that we ask of business leaders as we get started on the path of solution selling:

> *What few things absolutely must go right for you to achieve your most important business objectives?*

This question has served us well for decades. It is a broad but clear request to learn the most important priorities (sometimes called critical success factors) of the customer organization. Once we hear these headlines – e.g., "reduce employee turnover by 10 percent," "improve inventory turns by 12 percent," and "reduce bad debt by 5 percent" – we have the opportunity to follow up with questions seeking the specific plans the customer has in place to achieve these objectives.

The wording of this thoughtful question has been carefully chosen. We are asking our prospect, preferably a person of authority in the business, to focus on the small handful of priorities that *must go right* for the company to be successful. The business leader will typically name from two to five major priorities. Once the customer has laid out his most important business priorities, we follow up with a simple line of questioning:

> *What specific people, resources, plans, or projects do you have in place to make these priorities happen?*

This urges the customer to dive to a level deeper in his business, to specifically detail plans and programs that will make these "few things that must go right" become reality. It will be evident if the plans are a bit thin or are incomplete. The customer's answers to this line of questioning will become crucial to us as we structure our solutions or offerings to help him achieve these most important priorities.

Once the customer has shared these most important business priorities and specific plans and programs aimed at achieving them, it is time to begin the process of becoming a trusted advisor to the customer's business. We do this, not by immediately shooting our product proposal at the customer, but rather by positioning the functional highlights of our business solutions and asking the customer for the opportunity to work with his key business leaders to tailor a set of solutions aimed at fortifying his most important business priorities. We do not talk about our price at this point. Rather, we promise that our solutions will positively impact our customer organization's ability to serve *their* customers and boost our customer's profitability.

Sales professionals sometimes protest that the process of discovering the customer's priorities and structuring a tailored solution takes too much time and prolongs the sales cycle. We vehemently disagree with that short-sighted sentiment. We are convinced that we become indispensable partners to our customers when we work this way. We form "customer for life" partnerships when they understand that we have their best interests at heart because we live the principle that *"My success can only follow the success of my customer!"*

26 Selling Strategically

Strategic selling is one of the buzz-phrases of our times.

Furthermore, strategic selling is currently one of the most misused, least understood concepts in the profession, as we saw in a recent experience with a customer. While we were assisting her in conducting an account review of one of her largest accounts, the sales rep stated that her strategy for this account was "To be the sole provider for all of the products and services they provide." This clearly is not a strategy. It is at best a long-term goal for her company and certainly not her customer's interest.

Salespeople overuse the word *strategy* in their presentations and reports to upper management, in hopes that management will think they have thought through what their approach is in managing a key account or pursuing a specific complex sales opportunity.

To paraphrase Albert Einstein, things should be as simple as possible, but no simpler. To that end, we want to debunk some false thinking about selling strategically and provide a simplified, disciplined approach to this critical element of being a consummate sales professional.

Strategy, defined simply, is setting course and direction. In selling there are two primary reasons for applying strategy:

- To grow an account within a specific time frame, e.g., a year.
- To win a specific sales opportunity. This is most often applicable for long sales cycles that are complex and competitive.

Successful salespeople apply strategy at three levels: to an Account, to an Opportunity, and to a Sales Call. The key to working strategically at each level is to ensure your strategy is integrated – your efforts must synchronize.

- Account management involves developing an understanding and a plan for the customer's business to enable you to identify the portfolio of opportunities that will have the greatest impact on both the customer's and your own business.

- Opportunity management means using a disciplined approach, supported by specific selling strategies that will significantly increase your ability and likelihood of winning individual sales opportunities.
- Sales calls management is the plan for making each sales call effective for the customer and for your organization. Our aim is always to lift the effectiveness of our customer's organization while creating competitive advantage for our company.

In the next two chapters we will explore these various levels and applications of strategy in selling and help distinguish strategy from tactics. Let's start with a little context:

The use or misuse of the word *strategy* most often starts with senior management. Managers use product or pricing promotions to boost sales or move costly inventory, and position the activity as a *strategy* to achieve a sales revenue plan. But these are simply reactions to short-term problems of "making the numbers" – and thus they are *tactics*. Calling them strategies creates confusion throughout the sales ranks.

Another problem develops when sales managers send conflicting messages to the field, such as:

- Sell consultatively (strategy)... but promote this product, feature, or service now (tactic).
- Sell value rather than price (strategy)... but offer this one-time, special deal (tactic).

At first glance, one would think that at least the customer benefits from all of these mixed signals and broken sales plays. Yet most customers are seeking a supplier and salesperson who truly understands their needs. Customers need sales professionals who help them solve their business problems through specific solutions that establish a value which is customer-based, rather than supplier-driven.

Though we may feel threatened at times by non-strategic competitors who merely live on product promotions and bag-diving sales reps, in the long term, the strategically motivated sales organization has a decided advantage in achieving competitive advantage.

27 The Get-Real Approach to Account Management

Account management involves developing an understanding and a plan for the customer's business so you can identify the portfolio of opportunities that has the greatest impact on both your customer's and your business.

Sales professionals leverage the account plan by sharing it with the relevant executive in the customer's organization. Strategy becomes a collaborative process and builds strong relationships within the account.

When properly created, an account plan teaches customers something about their business. The key elements of an account plan are:

- Defining the customer's business issues and goals.
- Understanding the customer's competitive challenges and opportunities.
- Being vividly clear on the customer's critical success factors, *those few things that absolutely must go right* for your customer to achieve his most important objectives.
- Building relationships within the customer's political environment.
- Identifying potential sales opportunities with the customer.

It is important and gratifying to conduct Account Planning semi-annually or annually for your key customers and prospects, from four perspectives:

1. The customer gets an external, professional assessment of his or her organization's business challenges and opportunities.
2. Your organization gets to increase the value of its offering to the customer and the customer's customers by exploring how your product and service solutions really do serve them.
3. The customer spends more time with you, sharing more information with you than with your competitor – a significant advantage.
4. Finally, you gain a strategic advantage over competitors by sharing the account plan with relevant executives of the customer's organization.

Other sellers will appear more limited or mercenary, unless they invest in a similar manner.

All of this reinforces the importance of the sales role and provides the foundation for basing your strategy on the S.E.L. approach.

28 The Get-Real Approach to Opportunity Management

Opportunity management means using a strategic approach complete with specific selling strategies that will significantly increase your likelihood of winning business.

Within major accounts, most often there are several opportunities to pursue throughout a normal sales year. Sales professionals realize that each opportunity must be treated as a unique situation which must be considered on its own merits. In this chapter, we want to acknowledge the work of our colleague Dr. Steve Bistritz, of Learning Solutions International.

The key elements of opportunity planning are:

1. Assessing and prioritizing the potential opportunities.
2. Determining the customer's decision process for each opportunity.
3. Profiling key stakeholders who influence or make the decision for each opportunity, i.e., the political environment.
4. Developing selling strategies that support the sales objective and competitive threats.
5. Creating a plan that outlines the specific steps for a sales campaign, including the tactics and resources you must deploy properly in order to win the sales opportunity.

Each of these five elements is essential to approaching complex sales opportunities. So let's look at each element in turn.

Assessing and prioritizing the opportunity helps you separate opportunities from wishes or hopes. It is based upon answering a fundamental question: Is this opportunity one in which I can truly compete – and win – and will it be worth the effort? This requires you to make sure that you truly want to devote your time and your company's resources to pursue the sale.

Next, carefully consider the second and third elements, the customer's decision-making process and key influencers, from both formal and informal perspectives. You need to be aware that the ultimate selection is usually made by a few people who most influence the ultimate decision maker. We will address this topic further in Chapter 31.

This brings us to the fourth element: sales strategy. It's at the heart of the matter in winning blocks of business that are significant to both your customer and your company. True sales professionals work with their company resources and sales teams to devise selling strategies that out-think and out-maneuver their competitors.

In the *Art of War*, Sun Tzu speaks about the origin of strategy:

> *Know yourself, know your enemy and you need not fear one hundred battles. Know only yourself and not your enemy, and for every victory gained you shall sustain defeat. Know neither yourself nor your enemy, and you shall succumb in every battle.... The key to victory is not in defeating the enemy, but in defeating the enemy's strategy; therein lies their vulnerability.*

We can derive three key rules from this lesson. First, work hard to know what your competitor's sales strategy is. Ask yourself:

1. Does the competition have an advocate inside the customer's organization who will be significant to this sales campaign? If yes, what role does this person play in the decision-making process?
2. Does the competitor's offering create a special advantage for the customer that your solution does not? If yes, how will the competitor leverage it?
3. Is the competitor the current incumbent, and if so, is their position a strong one, or are they vulnerable? Have they caused the customer problems with their product or service?

To create a winning sales strategy, temporarily set aside your natural focus on your own solution, and assess the customer and the competitive landscape to identify any land mines that the competitor or his internal champions could install that would threaten your success for this specific sales opportunity. Once you've assessed the competitive situation, you will be prepared to devise a winning sales strategy and a tactical plan to successfully execute this strategy.

An imperative for deriving the appropriate strategy is to be vividly clear about what your sales objective is. This may seem evident - you may think that the goal is simply to win the sale. Yet we suggest that you think more deeply, because your objective declares what you want to win. For example, if the competitor is a strong incumbent, your objective in this opportunity may be to simply get your product in the door, to establish a *beachhead* inside the customer organization. The beachhead strategy aims to win a small piece of the customer's business, giving you the chance to establish your great service and products. Or, if your competitor has a distinct advantage in reputation, size, relationship or price, your objective could be to outmaneuver or neutralize the competitor's advantage. Being clear on your sales objective is key to choosing a winning sales strategy.

Finally, the fifth element of opportunity management: you need to have a plan. There are four general approaches to opportunity management.

1. *Direct*: If your solution, or your company, has an overwhelming competitive advantage, then go straight ahead and close the sale quickly and completely, before your competitor can even get any footing with the customer.
2. *Indirect*: Deploy this approach when the competition has a competitive advantage that cannot be defeated head-on. This requires you to counter their advantage with one of your own, or to find a way to change the customer's conventional thinking and help her accept a different, unique approach that will solve her problem through a solution that differs from your competitor's. It's sometimes known as "change the game."
3. *Segment:* Use this approach when the competitor is a strong incumbent. Simply attempt to get your product into the customer's organization, even in a limited way, with the longer-term plan of further penetrating the account once you have some footing. This is the "Establish a Beachhead" approach.
4. *Reposition:* We consider this a fallback strategy because you deploy it only when you don't think that you have a solution or strategy that can win

right now. With this approach, you try to get the customer to postpone the purchase or reconsider what his real needs are. This enables you to better position your company or solution to win.

As you can see, there is much more to actually winning a sale than simply presenting your company's solution and going for the close. Mastering these different sales strategies and knowing when to use each approach is a critical skill for every successful sales professional.

29 Being Strategic on Every Sales Call

Some sales reps may think that having a strategy for every call is taking the concept of strategy to a trivial level. Yet if you are not strategic and purposeful at the sales execution level, all of your strategic sales-call planning is meaningless. When you are strategic, you are prepared with both a short- and long-term purpose for every sales call or customer interaction as you execute a sales campaign. Three key elements will help you make your sales- call planning truly strategic:

1. Develop and track a tactical action plan for every customer interaction you have, emphasizing your value proposition, not price. That is, emphasize how you will make your customer more profitable, not what your product costs.
2. Execute the sales strategy, with specific sales call strategies and tactics, in every interaction with the customer - especially for the discovery call. Each team member must be clear what his or her role is and who their key contacts are within the customer organization. Establishing credible relationships will optimize each step of the sales campaign, especially during the discovery phase.
3. Leverage the consultative sales process and drive the S.E.L. concept throughout the sales campaign. The overall success of opportunity management is directly related to how flawlessly you and your team execute it and how well you demonstrate your belief that your success can only follow the customer achieving their business objectives.

Sales call management is the plan for making each sales effort effective and creating competitive advantage at the front line of the sales process.

Back to Einstein: These elements of selling strategically – at the account, opportunity, and call management levels – are as simple as possible, and no simpler. It's relatively easy to create them, yet really challenging to execute well. But it's worth mastering them. If you are strong in these strategic skills, you will drive long-term sales success.

30 👎 Not Real:
The Personal Relationship Trap

Often sales reps rely only on their personal relationships as their leverage to get business deals approved. However, unless your contact is actually the senior manager who has the formal responsibility to make such decisions, this approach can be a trap.

One risk of relying on personal relationships is that your contact may be at best only a mid-level influencer, or worse, merely a user of your product or service. This contact could have an inaccurate view of the politics inside his own organization, and may have little or no credibility with the formal decision-maker. Even worse, the formal approver could be an executive who is aligned with a competitive supplier or have one he simply likes better. That can create contention between the decision-maker and your contact.

Furthermore, sales reps often rely on their personal contacts to get their products approved. Yet no one can sell your solution better than you. Also, depending too heavily on a personal relationship to represent your influence in the account is risky. Should the person change roles or leave the organization, your connection can be challenged or destroyed.

If the personal relationship tactic fails, you are left with far less effective sales tactics, such as pushing your product's features or functionality and discounting price to try to save the opportunity.

31 Understanding and Leveraging the Politics in Your Customer's Organization

Successful salespeople understand how buying decisions are made and who really makes them.

Contrary to what one might guess, large buying decisions are not always made by the most senior executive in the customer's organization. Certainly spending large sums often requires approval by presidents and CEOs, or even by the board. However, real decision-making happens in both formal and informal ways.

Formal approval is generally made by the person we call the "most relevant executive." You can generally figure out who this executive is by asking, "Who has the most to gain or lose by making this business decision?"

Identifying this executive is important, because it helps you to discover who is a member of the relevant executive's informal decision-making group. Executives who have succeeded over time usually rely on a group of two to four people they know and trust. This inner circle has significant influence on the executive, regardless of the title or rank. Placed both inside and outside the organization, they may or may not have formal "position power." This explains why the informal approval often supersedes the formal process of decision making. These trusted advisors have experience the relevant executive depends on to make good business decisions. For the relevant executive, price, though always important, is less important than the value of the solution and the reliability of its provider.

Understanding how important buying decisions are *really* made will allow you to gain real competitive advantage for your sales strategy.

32 Presenting the Solution

As much as we would like our customer to excitedly buy our product or solution while we are in the midst of describing how it works, the reality is that we typically must go through a logical process to effectively advocate on behalf of our proposed solution. Though our customer may just ask for a price, we should create the opportunity to present the complete solution to give ourselves the best chance to win the customer's business. Here is the presentation methodology used by truly consciously competent sales professionals:

1. *Purpose – Process – Payoff (PPP)*. It is very important to make a habit of starting by describing why we are meeting and what we intend to solve (purpose). Then describe what will take place in this meeting, e.g., "Today I'll give you an oral presentation, a product demonstration, and then we can discuss implementation details" (process). Finally, grab the customer's interest and attention by hinting at the benefits your customer can gain by implementing the solution that you are about to detail (payoff). A solid PPP will provide a compelling opening to the meeting and give the customer reason to focus on the task at hand. It is also an opportunity to get immediate positive feedback by simply asking, at the end of the PPP, "How does that sound?" We want the customer to get into the habit of agreeing with us right from the beginning!

2. *Current State*. Summarize the situation as described by your customer. Here is where the customer should be reminded of the problematic situation that will ultimately be resolved by our solution. As you step through this current state, the customer should be nodding in agreement and recognition that you have a good understanding of their situation. Close this section of your presentation with vividly clear statements of the problem(s) your customer faces. You can be sternly serious about the negative impacts of the problems, but give hints of optimism that there is a solid resolution to those problems – which you are about to reveal.

3. *Description of Solution*. Once your customer has agreed that you have a

clear, correct picture of the current situation, you have an open path to move to your solution. In keeping with the very solid concepts offered by our friends at Wilson Learning, we advocate the use of a three-step process to describe your solution: *Solution – Advantage – Benefits*. First describe your *Solution* by vividly but concisely noting what it is and how it works. Don't dive into feature details, but instead calmly state how your solution will change the currently flawed situation.

Interestingly, most of your competitors will stop at this point. They assume that the customer will infer how the solution will solve the problem. But you must do more to assure you leave nothing important to chance! After describing the solution, address the S.E.L. *Advantages*, namely, how it will provide improved service for your customer's customers, how it will positively affect the economics of your customer's situation, and how it will improve her quality of work life. Use terms such as profit, cost reduction, elimination of waste, simplicity, and customer service enhancements. Finally, speak in terms of the *Benefits* – the positive impacts on the customer's business and/or her life that she will experience as a result of your solution. We will help the long term success of the business by providing greater control, a more predictable set of business processes, risk reduction, and other appeals aimed at giving the customer the feeling that she is gaining control and truly running her business, not that it is running her, once she implements your solution!

4. *Ask for questions.* It is important for customers to talk at this point. They will doubtless have questions, concerns, doubts, and worries. You want to surface these potential objections *now* so that you can deal with them in the moment. If you treat objections as "buying signals," it will help you resolve them to your customer's satisfaction and lead invariably toward agreement.

5. *Implementation.* Concisely describe your implementation plan. To many, implementation details seem boring and unnecessary. But this step serves several highly valuable purposes. As you describe dates, times, accountabilities that you will take on and clarify those required from your customer, you will be able to see where you stand by observing her reactions. If your customer actively participates with lots of good ques-

tions, then you know that she is seriously considering your proposed solution. If you see disinterest, it is a fairly safe bet that she is just "shopping around" and not taking you seriously, at least at the moment. Sharing your implementation plan is also an opportunity to show the true capabilities of your business. If you are strong in our business fundamentals it will come across in the implementation discussion. This discussion should very solidly differentiate you from your competitors, who will typically take this step for granted if they prefer to talk about product features and pricing promotions. Finally, if the implementation discussion goes well, with lots of head nods, approving remarks, and positive comments, it is a perfect time to *ask for the customer's agreement* to move forward.

6. *Close.* Ask permission to move forward with your proposal. As we just noted, we recommend asking for the sale as a natural extension of the implementation discussion. When your groundwork is done well, closing is just a "dot" in the process of selling, not the mammoth step it's made out to be in most sales seminars and books. The close is a very natural step. It is not a moment to try "trick" your customer. Rather, as an honest person asking to move forward and improve the customer's business through the adoption of your solid solution, it's a moment for agreement.

33 👎 Not Real: The Myth of Magic Closes

The most overrated concept of selling is the notion of a "great closer." If you do a Google search on *Closing the Sale*, you will find over 43 million entries! There are entire textbooks, CDs, DVDs, and all manner of training courses solely devoted to the topic of closing. But despite the macho aura that some attach to it, closing is not an exercise in toughness or a badge of courage. Rather, closing is simply the natural outcome of the rest of the sales process done well.

We were struck by one offer on a book jacket: "Learn the 24 most ruthless closing tactics that can turn even your most hard-nosed prospects into cash-generating customers." If we see our jobs as tricking our customers into buying from us through the use of catchy phrases or somehow maneuvering our customers into doing something they really do not want to do, we have seriously missed the mark. If we spend our self-development time drilling endlessly on how to "ask for the sale" in a strong-armed way, we will not maximize our personal development. If we think that customers buy because of the way we ask for the sale, we misunderstand how people buy. Yes, we *must* ask for the sale. But we must also understand that customers buy when we solve their problems, *not* when we come up with a catchy way to get them to say yes!

Often times sales representatives believe that being a slick negotiator is also part of closing. This concept ranges from seeking ways to compromise on such things as price or features, to being able to manipulate the customer into accepting what is possible. This approach is a win-lose game.

There is nothing magic about closing if we have done the groundwork that naturally leads to a decision. The myth of tricky closing techniques that will lift sales is just that – a myth. In a business setting when you are dealing with professional decision-makers, this over-emphasis on the emotion and phrasing of "the close" is wasted effort. Business professionals want to see what our products and services will do for their bottom line. If we cannot show positive impacts on their profit and loss sheet, there is no magic close that will win the business.

34 The Art of Get-Real Closing

In the sales management community you often hear people say, "We are just looking for closers." The Real point of view, however, is that closing should be the simplest part of the sales process. If we take the approach that *my success can only follow the success of my customer,* then the skill of closing the deal becomes very simple. We reject the belief that we should trick our customer into buying by using some form of ruthlessly effective close.

In today's business-to-business selling world, we *arrive at the close* of the selling opportunity after discovering the flaws in the customer's business that will be addressed by or eliminated with the installation of our solution. Once we clearly articulate our *Solution* by professionally identifying it, pointing out the *Advantages* of changing the way the customer does business, and showing the clear *Benefits,* we can close the sale with such statements as:

- Are you ready to get started?
- With your agreement, we will begin the implementation next week.
- I would love the opportunity to move your business to my company. May I offer you a proposal?
- Are we in agreement on all key terms?

Closing becomes more of a conversation when there is a need to seek a solution and a value that can meet both party's expectations and capabilities. Wilson Learning's good friend, Dr. William Ury, found in his work entitled "Getting to Yes" that the purpose of negotiating is to seek a mutually beneficial solution that is acceptable by both parties. Ideally, this outcome starts in the discovery process (Chapter 24) and is further developed by expanding the options for an optimal solution.

When done well, a great close to the sales process will lay out the future for the customer. It will describe your solution in concise detail. It will contrast the advantages of going with your solution versus the disadvantages of staying with the status quo (or of going with a competitor). It will drive home the benefits to be gained in terms of S.E.L.:

- Quality of *Service* improvements to be enjoyed by your customer's customers as a result of implementing your solution.
- *Economic* improvement to the customer's business (e.g., either revenue improvement or cost reduction).
- Quality of *Life* improvements to be enjoyed by the customer's employees in and outside of work.

Yes, we do want closers, but we want sales professionals who discover opportunities to improve the business operation of their customers by bringing forth new solutions for them.

Part 3

Hidden Elements of Sales Professionalism that Will Make You Stand Out from the Rest

"There is a prescribed set of sales steps that, if followed with vigor and skill, will clearly differentiate YOU from everyone you compete against!"

In this section you will see the Get-Real focus on the importance of calling on executives. You'll learn tactics aimed at helping you present your solutions powerfully and persuasively. Metrics, goal-setting, and productive uses of technology round out this section.

35 The Triumphs of Calling on Executives

Most successful sales professionals consider themselves *Sales Executives*. They believe that having consistent, effective interactions with executives in the customer's organization is essential to helping them solve their customer's business problems or seize competitive opportunities.

Research indicates that senior executives most often become involved at two stages of projects. Dr. Steve Bistritz, founder of Learning Solutions International, has made some insightful observations in this regard.

Early on in a project, they:

- Help those involved gain clarity on the critical issues.
- Establish project objectives and strategy.
- Establish parameters, such as time frames, budgets, and supplier criteria.

Later on, executives may return to:

- Become involved in negotiations and approvals.
- Oversee the implementation.
- Establish metrics for success.

Our experience tells us that executives do not respond well when sales reps send marketing promotions as "door openers." These promotions do not usually get sales reps in the door, and they certainly do not aid in building a relationship. Executives look for sales executives who are trusted by people they themselves trust or who they see are aligned with their own goals and objectives.

Our sales experience clearly indicates four critical elements to meeting and exceeding senior executives' expectations:

1. Exhibit knowledge and understanding of your customer's organization's goals, objectives, business drivers, and challenges.

2. Ask the Magic Question: *What absolutely must go right for you to achieve your most important business objectives?* Offer fresh business perspectives, strategic thinking, and generate insights that connect your offerings to their business needs.
3. Advocate business solutions that become known within your customer's organization as offering a compelling value proposition aimed at the S.E.L. principles.
4. Demonstrate responsibility and show you can be held accountable.

To master the skills for gaining credibility and building trustful relationships with executives, you must at least meet and, better yet, exceed their expectations. You can do this if you embrace the approaches we've discussed in previous chapters. As a reminder, here they are:

1. S.E.L. – The three ways you can add value to your customers' business: help them enhance their Service-giving capabilities, enhance their Economics, and enhance the quality of work Life for their employees.
2. Selling On Purpose – The conviction that sales is a noble profession with a unique purpose, not just a job moving product. Professional salespeople can be among the most positive contributors to a society.
3. Being consultative in all things – having a never-ending thirst to understand your customer and find ways to enhance his business or his life with your solutions is the essence of your mission.

If you can earn the reputation of being an accountable business problem solver with the key leaders in your sales territory, you will develop and enjoy a sustainable competitive advantage with senior executives.

36 👎 Not Real: Are You Your Own Competition?

Sales professionals must accept certain realities about their world. One of them is that they are never going to win all the business to be had in their territory. Once that concept sinks in, they take a more strategic approach and identify the accounts where they are most likely to win.

Consider the concept of 30-40-30. Basically, about thirty percent of the potential accounts the sales professional has will always prefer to do business with him, for a variety of reasons. On the other hand, another thirty percent are accounts he probably never will win because those customers will choose the competition for some other variety of reasons. The remaining forty percent in the middle are up for grabs.

Many factors ultimately determine who wins those accounts, including those you've been reading about in this book. In addition, the way the sales professional thinks about his competitors directly influences how many of those forty-percent accounts he'll win for his company. Let's first explore the Not Real approach to dealing with the competition.

Everywhere he turns in his territory, the sales rep finds a competitor who might be very effective at winning and keeping business. At times, he may feel that the competitor has all the advantages, making him see himself as a David fighting the formidable Goliath. Even the sales professional who is actually a giant in his industry or market can feel plagued by lesser competitors who are nipping at his heels. Every day promises another hard battle, and selling starts to feel more like a war rather than a peaceful, honorable endeavor.

Over time, a sales rep can be affected by these realities, and unfortunately he may take on Not Real behaviors. Rather than acknowledging or accepting the fact that competition is real and healthy, the sales rep may act in ways that ultimately reflect badly on him. He might start bashing the competition, stretching or twisting the truth, or using false bravado to declare the competition doesn't even exist. Or he can fall into hating the competition, criticizing competitors to the point of being vengeful, hoping to lure customers away from their current vendors.

These behavior patterns usually prove ineffective and even detrimental for the sales rep. The salesperson who tries to raise his stature by putting his competitor down is seldom attractive in the eyes of the prospective buyer. Furthermore, by ridiculing the competition, he is indirectly criticizing the buyer's intelligence because the buyer was stupid enough to buy the competitors' goods and services in the past.

These approaches lead to two unproductive outcomes. The first reflects badly on the salesperson and makes him appear weak or unprofessional; the second pushes the customer over to the competitor's side. Neither approach leads to success in contentious sales situations.

37 Managing the Competition and Personal and Task Motives for Buying

The consummate professional respects her competitors. She recognizes that there are strong, reputable players on every team and they want to win as much as she does.

Sales professionals learn to leverage their company's strengths and its offerings against the competitor's vulnerabilities. On the other hand, a salesperson must manage the limitations of her company's own solutions. She will do this best by being vividly clear about what the customer truly needs and will invest in. At times this could require that, in the best interests of the customer, a sales professional may even need to *share the account* with the competition to take the best care of the customer.

When partnering with the competition appears to be the right thing for the *customer*, we have found that it is honorable to be the proactive provider in proposing such a solution. The customer will be inclined to look more favorably toward the sales professional who puts the customer's best interests ahead of his own desire to keep all the sales opportunities for her company.

Nevertheless, it is obviously ideal to keep what you have and then to win as many of the uncommitted forty-percent accounts as you can. The Real sales professional starts by protecting her current accounts against competitive threats. While securing those, she devises plans to win sales opportunities in situations in which the prospect's decision could go either way. She must leverage her solutions' strength against the competitor's weaknesses, doing so respectfully.

In order to win the majority of those sales that are up for grabs, we must keep our focus on the customers' interests, especially by discovering what is known as their *personal* and their *task motives*. These are some of the most critical real reasons that people chose one provider over another. An artfully phrased benefit statement will appeal to both the personal- *and* task-related motives of the customer.

There are four categories of personal motives: Power/Control, Recognition/Ego Enhancement, Comfort/Maintaining Harmony, and Accuracy/Being Right. The focus here is less on what the product or service does and more on what it will do for the buyer personally – for example, advance his career.

A sales professional who can uncover and make appeals to the customer's personal interests will go far toward creating sustainable competitive advantage. This emphasis also helps create a viable chance of becoming and continuing to be the dominant provider in her marketplace.

At the same time, we must also directly appeal to the task motives of our customer. We have to assure that our product will satisfy the functional issues in their business or personal situation that are causing problems. An example of a task motive is the desire to reduce bad debt through creative collections solutions.

In the end, by combining these approaches, you can reduce the feeling of threat from competitors and engage yourself in the positive, Real service to your customers that will win and keep their business.

38 👎 Not Real: A Typical Bad Proposal

We like to follow the business mantra that says, "Never leave anything important to chance! " Yet an unhappy reality of selling is that we sometimes work very hard to develop an opportunity, then fumble it away with a less-than-professional written document that advocates our proposed solution. Here are the elements of the typical bad proposal:

- Cover page – maybe there, maybe not, or if there, missing professional details and information
- Product feature descriptions
- Price of recommended product or service
- Contract

This skimpy document lacks the professional elements you will read about in a moment. Remember that your written document may be seen by people who have not met you yet and may have little or no awareness of the solution that you offer, after having done such a great job of developing in collaboration with your contacts. Your written proposal is yet another way to demonstrate your professionalism. Don't spoil your good work by delivering a second-rate document!

39 A Real Proposal:
Complete, Concise, Correct

We cannot always be physically present to advocate on behalf of our solution. Though our primary contacts may not need detailed documentation of our work together to develop a solution, it is a good bet that others in the organization will want to see the details in writing without meeting with us. In addition, we may be competing with others who are attempting to sell a similar solution to our customer. Proposals take on added importance as they sit on conference room tables in front of decision-makers who are weighing the pros and cons of competing solutions. For these and a host of other good reasons, it is very important to develop thoughtfully written proposals laid out in a logical fashion that will lead to the conclusion that *we* are the firm to choose.

Here is the most effective way to structure a Real written sales proposal, one that that will allow us to leave nothing important to chance *and* will sell on our behalf when we are not there in person. Our simple but effective structure leads to the obvious conclusion that the customer should shake hands and do business with you.

- *Cover Page:* A tasteful front cover identifies the document and makes clear who created it. Display both your and the customer's logos along with a concise title that describes the outcome of the proposal, like "Proposal to Improve XYZ Order Processing Efficiency." It is inappropriate to title the proposal with your product information – that will be done inside the document.
- *Table of Contents:* Simply note, with page numbers, each element of the proposal so that the reader can easily go to pages of interest without confusion or wasted effort.
- *One-Page Executive Summary:* Many people will only read your one-page executive summary and have a look at the pricing information later in the document. So concisely describe the problem, the solution, the

advantages gained by the customer, the terms, and the plan of implementation in this summary. This page is *the* most powerful element of your written document.

- *Discovery Agreement Summary:* In this section, concisely detail the situation that will be positively affected by your solution. This is where the customer should hear his own voice and terminology as you summarize the issue(s) that will be solved with the adoption of the proposed solution.

- *Summary of the Solution:* Name your solution and describe in appropriate detail how the problem(s) described in the discovery section will be positively impacted by our solution. It is appropriate to describe meaningful details of our solution in this section, though it is seldom appropriate to delve deeply into product features and functions. (That is more appropriate for optional appendix reading at the end of the proposal).

- *Statement of Benefits:* Clearly state the S.E.L. advantages the customer will gain by implementing your proposed solution. Detail Service improvements for our customer (and/or *his* customers). Also describe the Economic benefits your customer will gain from your proposed solution. Finally, describe improvements to the quality of work Life your customer will enjoy as a result of implementing your solution.

- *Implementation Plan:* Describe the *what, how, when,* and *by whom* aspects of implementing the solution that you propose. Your customer wants details that give him or her the peace of mind that your organization will deliver on-time, top-quality service or products in every step of the implementation.

- *Terms and Conditions:* You provided the economic benefits of the solution in the Statement of Benefits section. Here you detail the actual price elements and contract terms. Make certain to include an executable contract in every proposal, so it can be approved on the spot, in the event that objections are cleared and the customer is ready to move on your recommendation.

- *Appendix:* Use the appendix for optional items that are not critical to sell the solution but which help the customer who wants to dig deeper to get at the details. Product brochures, technical specifications, references from satisfied customers, contact information of key personnel who will be involved in the implementation are typical. Other details that should not be orally presented but may be desirable in the document can also be included here for the more analytical reader.

These nine elements don't mean you need a wheelbarrow to deliver it. Length is a function of the complexity of your offering. Just ask yourself if your proposal is complete, concise, and correct, and stop writing when you can answer yes. Then look it over for visual impact. (Is the type easily readable? Do you use white space, formatting, and color to aid comprehension and help skimmers?). Finally, spell check, let it rest, have a colleague read it, correct it, and present it to your customer. You'll know you've done a Real, good job.

40 👎 Not Real: The Myth of Forecasting

Sales leaders spend a great deal of time thinking about sales forecasting. Weekly meetings close with everyone's performance forecast. Monthly reports and meetings dwell on the elements of each sales professional's pipeline of opportunities. Quarterly reviews ensure that every person in the organization is doing all he or she can to "bring in the number."

Yet all this activity, aimed at reviewing opportunities and predicting the future, can cause dysfunctional behavior among salespeople.

- "I only put it in my forecast if I'm dead sure it's going to close. I don't want management constantly bugging me about my likelihood to close on opportunities that I am just exploring."
- "I don't like forecasting my results any sooner than I absolutely have to. In my company Finance gets hold of this information and builds the projected sales into the following year's revenue plan, robbing me of the up-side I would otherwise gain from a good sale."
- "I have two forecasts – one for management, that is relatively sparse, so as to cut down on the questions like, 'When is the Larson deal going to close?' and one for myself that is my actual forecast of what I will be able to sell."
- "I throw everything but the kitchen sink into my sales pipeline forecast so that management knows I'm out there in the marketplace pushing for opportunities wherever I can. I'm not very accurate with my forecast but I get lots of kudos for pursuing a wealth of opportunities."

Done right, sales forecasts are extremely useful and important. If they are based upon an honest assessment of opportunities in the marketplace and not used as a weapon by management, they can be very important coaching and predictive tools for the mature sales organization. If they are used improperly they become a waste of time, a mammoth source of dissatisfaction for all involved, and quite possibly, a very bad read on where the business is going.

41 Sales Forecasting Done Well

We strongly believe in the following practices as appropriate with regard to sales forecasting:

- Each sales professional should have an Opportunity Board. The first column lists all the relatively unqualified "opportunities" that you will explore over the next 60 days. Moving to the right are columns that show sales progress (see below). A healthy pipeline should have sales opportunities in each column. You should only make a forecast on opportunities that are in the proposal and decision columns. (We would like to thank our friend Stephen Schiffman, who has written over 40 books on professional selling, for his mentorship on this important topic.)

Opportunity Board						
Opportunities	Current Actions	Discovery	Qualified Opportunity	Proposal Stage	Decision Stage	Imple-mentation
Blackstone Inc. Series 44 or 56?	1st meeting 1 October	X				
Agate Hill Part 55G or 214Y	Checking our pricing with vendors; proposal due 10 October		X			
Sanchez Co-op Part 214Y	Deliver proposal 15 November			40K to 50K units @ $ 72.50		
D'Antonio Part 77LS	Decision 20 November				38,000 units @ $65.80	
Chen and Son Part 86R	Start installing 1 December					82K units @ $77.89

- *Sales managers should not penalize high performers by attempting to use their sales forecasts as evidence that they should carry higher sales goals.* We strongly believe that high performers should *not* carry higher sales achievement goals than low performers. Sales should not be like golf, where handicaps are given based upon different skills. Leading salespeople shouldn't be penalized! Differential goals should be based on opportunities in the different selling territories, not on the skills of the salespeople. This view may seem controversial to some sales managers but it should not be. Why would we want to penalize our most successful producers by effectively making them make less money per sales transaction? Why would we want to make it more difficult for them to achieve "President's Club" status than the more marginal performer? Sales professionals are extremely conscious of perceived injustices. In our view, the best performers are worth their weight in gold. They sometimes accomplish the work of two or three marginal performers. Sales managers should do all they can to assure that the sales environment promotes above-normal production, not punishes it.
- Only the sales manager who is directly responsible for a salesperson should conduct regular sales pipeline reviews. He or she should build trust with the salesperson so the forecast supports a viable process for assessing opportunities. If senior leaders are brought into the process, the process tends to unravel because salespeople start feeling that their careers are on the line. If senior leaders want to see the sales pipelines, they should conduct such reviews with the sales management team. "Drop-in leadership" can be more troublesome than it is worth. This is not to say that senior leaders do not have the right to drop in – they do. They should leave the detailed questioning about week-to-week pipelines to the people who are actually looking at them each week.

To enhance your forecasting, take advantage of some of the great pipeline tools that are built into such sales management systems as Siebel, Interaction, Salesforce.com and the many other customer relationship management systems that are in the marketplace.

42 Numbers: Metrics that Matter

There is an interesting dilemma for the consciously competent, Real sales professional who wants to truly understand the metrics that drive performance: *The achievements that companies pay variable compensation for often do not really measure sales process success or failure.* Rather, the variable compensation plans of most sales organizations really are just a scoreboard that reflects the *final results* of selling. They are not particularly helpful for the sales manager who wants to get a good handle, weekly or monthly, on the effort, efficiency, and effectiveness of his sales professionals.

Given that the final sales result does not always give a complete explanation for sales success or failure, we must dig down and discover those measurable behaviors that are indicators of a sales professional really driving her business. The most reasonable way to discover *metrics that matter* is to do some reverse engineering. Take a look at sales you have made in the past and dissect them to understand key points in the process of the sale. Understand the *who*, *what*, and *how* of the sales made in your organization. If your product line is broad or complex, it is likely that you will want to take several angles on this analysis. Perhaps you will break down sales by:

- Geographic area
- Product line
- Industry
- Price point
- Contract length

The important thing is to discover the elements in the sales process that must go right for you to be successful. Keep a keen eye out for things that can be counted or measured, as these will help you build up the true *metrics that matter*. Below are examples of measurable elements most commonly used by thoughtful sales leaders who want to measure more than just the end results:

- Steps in the sale – Discover the phases that a sale typically passes through on the way to completion (e.g., introduction and relationship establishment; discovering currently unmet needs; presenting a solution; sales evaluation and approval process; implementation of solution).
- Number of prospects actively being worked on – This will help get a sense of the number of opportunities it takes to achieve your objective. Ultimately you can calculate your "sales success average," a measure of your success rate per opportunity. This is a key insight you must get to in order to avoid the cross-your-fingers-and-hope mode of selling.
- Revenue in play per opportunity – An important measure that gives a sense of the value of opportunities "in play" that you are working on. Though it is difficult to apply a potential revenue value early in the sales process, it is important to place a prospective value on every opportunity as you move through the sales process.
- Number of appointments – This is a controversial measure that we all look at with cynicism. It is not a measure of effectiveness in any way. Rather, it is a measure of effort, of "getting out there." Many sales professionals say, "Don't count my appointments – count my results." True enough, but we do need to know the average number of appointments or meetings required to regularly achieve one's selling objectives.
- Contracts on Desks (CODs) – A measure of proposals currently being considered by customers, it is used to get a sense of the possibilities of sales closures in a given territory. A lack of CODs is a definite warning sign of underperformance. Conversely, a very high COD count is not necessarily a measure of greatness (especially if the sales professional is just churning out offers with minimal needs discovery time with the prospective customers).

There is no question that it is critically important for the sales professional and her management to establish key measurable elements that drive the sales process and serve as indicators of successful performance. It is equally crucial that we settle on the right metrics: the *metrics that matter!*

43 The Secret of Get-Real Goal Setting

A chapter on sales goal setting might seem out of place in a book that is primarily intended for sales representatives. However, given that a sales goal is a vitally important topic to every sales professional, we want to shine some light on what sales management goes through in developing goals. We also want to share our views on some dos and don'ts of good goal-setting practices. Many of the things we note below are factors in goal setting that require thoughtful leadership to go against the grain of what many companies consider accepted goal-setting practices. We hope this insider viewpoint on the challenges of goal setting will help you gain a greater understanding of how goals are set.

There are several challenging factors that must be weighed in goal setting as well as some pitfalls to avoid:

- Sometimes sales leaders try to be too perfect in goal setting. This is counterproductive. Endless analysis aimed at getting just the right number and assuring that every single territory has its own customized goal is a trap to avoid. A far better approach employed by many good sales leaders is the concept of goal ranges. This means that, based upon territory capabilities, there should be medium, large, and jumbo territory goals, not 400 different goals for 400 territories.
- Do a great job building appropriate territories based on territory capacity, using these three goal categories. For example: Texas may be a superb state for selling your products. It has lots of prospects, your products are a perfect fit, and you see a solid history of performance across multiple sales professionals. Texas should have some "jumbo" territory goals. On the other hand, Louisiana may not be such a good fit for your company. It may have many fewer prospects and not as many applications for your products. You would place the "medium" territory goal on a Louisiana territory.
- Setting goals based upon prior year performance in a territory is typically a bad approach. It may be logical, from an analytical point of view,

but it is not fair or motivating. Goal setting done this way infuriates top performers and rewards poor ones. We do not believe in punishing sales professionals for having had a great prior year. Instead, great performers should be rewarded for driving hard all year long, calm with the knowledge that they will not be penalized with a higher goal next year *just because they are good.*

- Don't goal the performer – goal the territory! Great performers want the freedom to go prove their greatness every year. As long as they perceive that their goal is relatively fair, they will continue to drive great performance year after year. The last thing an organization should do to superstars is challenge them with higher and higher goals because they excel and can "take more goal." This mistake is one of the leading reasons why star performers leave your company for the chance to be a star elsewhere.

44 👎 Not Real: Performance-Draining Uses of Technology

Despite some of the great technology tools available, we are not 100 percent sold on the universal benefits of technological innovations in our lives. Below are some aspects of technology enhancements that concern us.

- *E-mail Smokescreens* – Sending e-mail messages that are unnecessary and using them to avoid live contact are self-deceptions that sales professionals must avoid. Creating an e-mail message is as simple as breathing for most of us. That does not automatically make it a good thing to do. Business professionals should think carefully when using electronic mail as a substitute for live conversation. We are particularly skeptical about people who think they are selling by creating and sending e-mail messages to customers and prospects. There is seldom a better alternative to communicating live – at least by telephone. We shake our heads when we see "e-mail campaigns" developed and executed, with the sales rep then sitting back to await the response!
- *The Conference Call* – Telephony has made great leaps forward in another way besides mobile phones, particularly with the ability to easily conduct a conference call among a handful or hundreds of people. There are some fantastic uses of this technology, generally modeled around concise sharing of important information. What we have observed, however, is the "stay in the home office" mentality of many sales managers who feel they are doing a good job of communicating and being with the troops as long as they have frequent conference calls. What they often fail to see is that these regular calls can become a ball and chain that their people dread, make fun of, and multi-task their way through.

An irony about the *paperless, computer-based society:* Mead Paper (since purchased by Westvaco) bought into the computing business in 1973 when the CEO bought what became LexisNexis, an electronic information company that serves the needs of law firms, corporations, law enforcement, and government. The ironic thing about this purchase was that the visionary former CEO of Mead thought that the growing computer boom would dramatically reduce the world's need for paper.

What he could not have foreseen was that computers on every desk, coupled with the invention of electronic mail, dramatically *increased* the use of paper. Literally hundreds of times more documents are created today that would not have been written just twenty years ago, thanks to the ease of word processing and e-mail. It is not at all uncommon for today's sales professional to receive 50 to 100 e-mails daily (not counting spam) and to send dozens of messages as well. Twenty years ago a sales professional might have received 5 to 10 documents in the mail daily and sent out a similar amount. Electronic mail has literally shot up the need to create and review documents twenty-fold for the average business professional.

Technology can be life changing in the positive effects it can bring to our lives – when used properly. When used improperly or sloppily, it can become a royal pain in the hindquarters. So Get Real – think carefully and get consciously competent about how you use technology in your work.

45 Positive, Performance-Enhancing Uses of Technology

I have spent the better part of the past three decades working for two major technology firms, AT&T and LexisNexis. I particularly appreciate how technology can change our lives for the better, when used properly. For example, I seem to have a particularly warm place in my heart for satellite systems. I have satellite television so that I can watch ALL of my beloved NFL football games. I have satellite radio in my car to assure that I always have 200 digital channels to listen to, no matter where I go. And a satellite-based GPS system, which has transformed me from a bumbling, get-lost-often driver to a smooth operator who is never lost. With it, I can get anywhere I want to go as long as I have a street address. Yes, when used properly, technology can dramatically improve our personal and work lives. Yet *used properly* is the key point. Here are our tips on the use of technology in the workplace, especially for sales professionals:

- *Cell phones:* This may be the greatest single invention for the field sales representative in the past 50 years. As someone who sold on the road in the 70's and 80s, I remember all of those wasted miles driving the highways with no connection to the rest of the world. I would stop intermittently at gas stations to use pay telephones to contact my customers, my co-workers, the home office, and my family. The cell phone makes us productive and accessible, no matter where we are. It enhances our ability to serve the customer, to stay in touch with people we depend on, and gives us the ability to "get work done" continuously. The rapidly developing world of smart phones allow us to do things never before imaginable such as text message, have complete access to our calendars, e-mail from anywhere, and share documents while on the go.
- *E-mail:* What an incredible innovation – and we already take it for granted. E-mail enables us to share vital information in written and visual form with anyone and everyone, instantaneously. We can efficiently cre-

ate and send letters, proposals, and contracts in the blink of an eye. Decision-making can be dramatically improved over the old days (can you recall when we had to go back to the office and create documents and then send them by snail mail?). E-mail is phenomenal for communicating important news, providing product specifications, updating the team on progress in an account, and for touching base quickly.

- *Electronic Faxing and Document Sharing*: We are much less hardware dependent than ever before. It is no longer necessary to purchase a fax machine to send and receive documents. You can now send and receive documents via services made to scan and share documents between people or groups. This can be used for contracts, photographs, or virtually any document type, avoiding the things that can go wrong with the sharing of "hard copy."
- *"Speak Up"*: Now normal versions of the Windows operating system allows you to dictate commands, lessening the need to type while maximizing your ability to think creatively!
- *Customer Relationship Management (CRM) software:* Siebel, Salesforce. com and a handful of other companies have created incredible tools designed to replace the old bulging manila folder and "bring-up file" or tickler systems of the past. Today's sales professional can easily keep track of every meaningful interaction with his customers and extended sales team through centralized CRM systems. This allows for much better team selling, better customer service, and a much more coordinated approach to the customer. It also can put some science into the sales forecasting aspect of our jobs, since most CRM systems have built-in sales pipeline management utilities. We highly recommend a very disciplined approached to customer relationship management, supported by a good CRM system.
- *Blackberry/PDA devices:* We cannot always have our laptop computer on and operating – it is just not appropriate or convenient. However, we can always have a mobile device that works as a cell phone available to compose, send, receive, and read e-mail and use for instant text messaging. The dramatic growth of these devices has changed the face of business. When people discuss the increased speed and pace of business, this portable communication device is normally at the center of the conversation. And *please*, use your hands-free, wireless microphone/earphone

(Bluetooth) when driving!

- *Global Positioning System (GPS) and Google Earth:* The ability to input an address into a device that then literally maps out where you want to go is an enormous leap forward for people who drive to customer locations. And if you aren't familiar with the geography you need to cover, Google Earth is invaluable. The price of GPS devices has come down dramatically over the past two years, making GPS available to all who need it. There is no longer an excuse for getting lost. The confidence that comes from knowing for sure where you are going and how long it will take you to get there is an incredible leap forward.

- *Flash memory drives:* These trusty little tools allow you to have a back-up presentation in case of corruption or loss of data, and makes using hotel business centers lots easier. (We carry all our major presentations on flash drives so that we can always be ready for opportunities *and* to protect against loss of information from our laptop computers' hard drives).

Keith Hawk

Part 4

The Bigger Picture in Professional Sales

"Selling and living on purpose requires you to be very clear about what your core beliefs and values are, and to have the personal and moral courage to cling to them, especially in times of challenge, doubt, and temptation."

We examine the traditional "Hunters vs. Farmers" debate in this section. It leads out toward a point of view about how we live our lives within the demanding world of selling and beyond, in our personal worlds. We challenge you to think about whether you are living On Purpose, and conclude with a self-survey to see how much you truly are doing so today.

46 👎 Not Real: "You Are Either a Hunter or a Farmer"

Conventional sales wisdom says that there are two main types of selling professionals:

1. The Hunter: A meat-eating, fun-loving, gun-slinging, high-living, Cadillac-driving, close-'em-at-any-cost salesdog.
2. The Farmer: A soft, cuddly, service-oriented, customer-loving, I-wanna-be-loved account manager.

This wisdom treats the skill-sets and personality traits of these types as if they were as different as night and day, as cats and dogs. Why is this conventional wisdom so prevalent? Let's examine some of the specific assumptions about the requirements of doing these two jobs that are presumed to be so different.

- *The Job of the Hunter:* A Hunter, in the profession of selling, is a salesperson who is supposed to go out, find, and close new accounts. The Hunter must be tough as nails, highly resilient, able to quickly find opportunities, and above all else, be a *closer* in that old-fashioned sense we debunked in Chapter 33.
- *The Job of the Farmer:* A Farmer is a salesperson assigned to work with existing accounts – a classic Account Manager. He must understand precisely what is going on within the account to ensure that the value of his product is being maximized, so that the customer would not seriously consider working with a competitor. The Farmer must also find opportunities for new applications for his products and services. He must develop relationships that serve his business well!

Two types – quite different, right? Or is that a bit of fiction?

45 Hunters and Farmers Are Not as Different as We Think!

We believe that great sales professionals typically have a healthy dose of *both* Hunter and Farmer characteristics and skills. Let's consider how we would create the Real salesperson, drawing a little DNA from both types.

The ideal new business development manager, a.k.a. the *Hunter,* is someone who can quickly understand the core purpose of her customer's business. She works consultatively to help the leaders within her customer firms make their business more efficient and profitable through the adoption of her products and services. If she does her job well, she is building customers for life, thanks to her ability to demonstrate how powerfully her company can help her customers be more successful.

The ideal account manager, a.k.a. the *Farmer*, will do a great job of seeing his customer base as a portfolio of opportunities to be prospected and "mined" for the constant development of new opportunities. If he works in this way he will always have a full slate of opportunities to grow his accounts in a healthy and prosperous way. He will use his powerful relationships and problem-solving skills to keep uncovering innovative new ways to satisfy his customers and make them want to keep doing more business with him.

When viewed in this fashion, we see that the differences between new business development professionals and account management professionals actually call on very similar skill sets:

- Business problem solving
- Relationship development
- Product applications knowledge
- The ability to move sales opportunities forward purposefully

Too often we typecast Hunters as fast-talking closers who just "get in and get out" of their accounts. The reality you discover when you investigate the work of powerful new account development salespeople is that they really are practicing the skills of seasoned account managers. They develop relationships. They uncover business problems within their prospect accounts. They present their solutions in ways that make sense to the customer.

We tend to typecast Farmers as people who want to give away the company in the name of providing good service to their accounts. Truth be told, the very best account managers are razor-sharp selling machines. They constantly uncover new selling opportunities within their accounts and advocate add-on customer buying for their firm in very powerful ways.

We conclude that these two breeds of sales professionals are not really very different from each other. A versatile, intelligent business problem solver, also known as a highly evolved sales professional, can play both roles at different times in his or her career. Though there are indeed shades of differences, the core skills that make strong sales professionals in both roles are largely similar.

48 Making Professional Relationships Work

Within most sales reps' lists of target accounts and prospects we find countless opportunities to utilize a consultative sales approach that will generate quota-busting business, working with the contacts that value a professional working relationship. Customers want trusted advisors who will help them solve their business problems and seize competitive advantage in their markets. These business leaders have families and lives that leave little time or interest for the old-school approach to business entertainment as the primary method for building a relationship.

So what does professional relationship selling consist of? When approached from a personal styles preference, Wilson Learning Worldwide provides data that clearly illustrates that salespeople, as a whole, only "connect" with about 25 percent of their customers and prospects. It is easier to sell to customers with whom they connect, simply based upon similarities of interests, communication, and overall comfort. No competent salesperson wants to automatically segment out 75 percent of his opportunities due to interpersonal style differences. We need strategies and tactics for dealing with the reality that we will not be perfect interpersonal matches with our target customers.

Building professional relationships requires a salesperson to have the versatility to quickly connect with every customer or new prospect by reducing the interpersonal tension that naturally exists at the beginning of a relationship. This enables the contact to comfortably answer questions and discuss their business issues, challenges, and needs. The salesperson no longer has to rely on small talk to carry the conversation, especially in the early stages of a new encounter. That seldom works anyway.

We suggest that you first identify the preferred behavioral style of the contact and temporarily adapt your own behavior to match that preference. For example, if the customer exhibits a very structured personal style with such evidence as a very neat office, minimal personal effects in the room, and very short, clipped statements, then it is unlikely that he will enjoy a long initial period of small talk on personal topics. You can recognize this style and get right to business.

Versatility – the ability to adapt to the style of your customer or prospect – will allow you to quickly put the contact at ease and move on to task-focused topics. This enables you to drive the discussions toward discovering and resolving business issues in an effective, efficient way. It elevates the level of interactions and, over time, the customer comes to rely on and reach out to you for help, because the customer respects the professional nature of your relationship. Often this relationship evolves into a more personal one as well, which further secures the business success, and provides for a mutually enriched life experience for the customer and you. (See *Versatile Selling* and *The Social Styles Sales Handbook,* by Wilson Learning Library, for more details on personal communication styles and versatility.)

49 👎 Not Real: Love 'Em and Leave 'Em!

Once the sale is made and the product or service is delivered, salespeople (especially those described as Hunters) often move on to the next "kill" and let the sales support people take care of the customer. Sometimes when that happens, the customer service or technical representative discovers that the salesperson has overstated the solution's capabilities or has promised additional free options or services beyond what the contract actually says was purchased. This re-draws the classic battle lines between Sales and Service, and the customer gets caught in the middle. That's not the ideal scenario for creating a positive customer experience. And it's not what Peter Drucker would recommend for *keeping* a customer (see Chapter 50).

For example: last week I called my satellite television service provider and excitedly upgraded to the newest high-definition digital video recording capability for my home television. The salesperson said it would be an "easy install" and I would soon be enjoying the ability to snappily record high-definition programs at the touch of a button.

When the service professional arrived at my house, he told me that the satellite dish I needed to access this service would be twice as big and 40 pounds heavier than the one now on my roof. He added that this new, bigger dish would probably blow off my roof in the next big wind. Further, he explained that it would require all-new wiring, which would mean drilling holes in my home's beautiful brick exterior.

When I asked why I did not get this information when I made the purchase, the service technician simply sighed, shrugged his shoulders and said, "You can't ever trust a salesperson who just sits on the phone to know how anything works!" Needless to say, this negative service experience greatly damaged my impression of his company. In fact, I cancelled the order and took my business to another provider.

This story illustrates the all-too-common tendency for sales reps to overcommit the use of the company's resources. Short-sighted reps want to give the customer too much for what the organization gets in return, or they minimize or ignore key facts that could be obstacles for the customer's decision to buy. We sometimes call this *reaching* – the process of over-promising and under-delivering. Reaching is an extremely short-term way to sell, one which causes service messes, not to mention hard feelings both within the organization and between the customer and the provider.

These negative customer experiences incline the sales rep to avoid his newly-acquired customer, just hoping that the customer will pay so he can collect his commission before things get too far out of hand. It's the classic love 'em and leave 'em scenario. This is *not* the way that Real sales professionals operate!

50 A Neglected Step in the Sales Process – Keeping Customers for Life

Peter Drucker describes the purpose of a business as finding customers and keeping them. We have always claimed that nothing happens until somebody sells something. It's one more reason why we contend that sales is the greatest profession. Your sale gives your company the opportunity to do whatever it is passionate about, including providing stakeholders with return on their investments, enabling many families to earn a living, and paving the way for all involved to fulfill their dreams.

That is why it is paramount that organizations take tremendous care of their customers once they are acquired. Research clearly indicates that it costs a company three to five times as much to find a new customer as it does to keep an existing one active. Salespeople should treat existing customers like they are the family jewels. Successful salespeople realize that developing a long-term relationship is worth the investment and that any committed relationship will have good times and hard times as well. So what can sales professionals do to keep these family jewels safe and secure? Let's explore a few best practices.

Leading salespeople know the implementation phase of a sale is critical. They check in as the implementation gets started so customers feel they are getting what they expected. Real sales professionals think through this phase and try to anticipate potential problems. Then they proactively direct their efforts and company resources to address those issues before they arise.

Still, no matter how hard you try to prevent problems, inevitably they will occur from time to time. When this happens, the Real sales professional stands out from the pack. Les Barker, a General Manager for Mead Merchants back in the 1970s and 80s, taught reps a valuable lesson in assuring post-sale satisfaction in a consultative sales training workshop. Les declared, "I actually *appreciate and value* the customer who is angry or upset with our company, the one who feels he is not receiving the quality or service he thought he purchased. I'll jump at that challenge, and work with that dissatisfied customer directly. Because once I solve the problem, they will become satisfied and even a little beholden to me. Then I will immediately sell them something else, and make darn sure they are happy with Mead and me. Ultimately, I will have gained one more customer for life!"

Our friends at Wilson Learning developed a process for addressing upset customers. To make it easy to remember, they use the acronym *LSCPA*, which stands for Listen-Share-Clarify-Problem Solve-Act. The process actually parallels the complete consultative sales approach. The sales professional who understands and employs this process will have truly mastered the skills and behaviors that *will* keep a customer for life!

51 👎 Not Real: Out of Balance, On the Edge

Imagine a time when you were crossing a creek or gully on a log. Perhaps you were trying to show off for a special friend, or you were on an excursion through the woods and really needed to cross there to avoid hiking a long distance out of your way to get to a safer crossing.

Picture yourself on that log above the abyss. Then recall the split-second when you started losing your balance: the fear that grasped you and made your knees weak, the loss of control and confidence that took your breath away, the dread of falling that sent your heart racing, the image of getting hurt blurring your real vision. Now push the pause button on this scene, with your body suspended in uncertainty! You get the picture?

Are you saying, "This is my life, every day!" as you read this?

Salespeople have their own set of challenges, finding and maintaining balance in their work life. Then they add in the demands of daily responsibilities that come with having a partner, children, extended family, church, community, civic duties – the list goes on and on.

Let's flash back to our log scene. To avoid falling, embarrassing, or injuring yourself, you instinctively drop to your knees and clutch the log, holding on for dear life. You either become paralyzed or you start inching forward – or worse, backward, choosing to retreat.

Isn't that what you find yourself doing in daily life as well? What does a loss of balance look like for a salesperson? Here are some indicators you may be experiencing:

- Stressed out: because of all the pressures, you feel very irritable, responding abruptly to customer calls and demands.
- Procrastinating: you make fewer sales calls, prospect inconsistently, and don't advance sales campaigns.
- Sloppy: you don't secure sales appointments due to lack of proper planning.

- Distracted: you multi-task while in the home office, putting off important assignments.
- Blaming: you fault the company and internal resources for not being able to satisfy customers or meet prospect requirements.
- Critical: you complain about the competition, because they are winning too often.
- Absent: you miss important events with your children and loved ones, blaming your absence on the demands of the job.
- Out of shape or sick: due to your lack of exercise (no time, no discipline) and poor diet (ditto, too much fast food).
- Escapist: you guiltily squeeze in fun activities, protesting, "I have to take time for myself!"
- Selfish: you ignore or decline church and community requests to contribute time and talents, mumbling, "I just don't have time."
- Tired and dissatisfied: you feel constantly exhausted (not getting proper rest and relaxation) and you are unfulfilled.

Can you see and feel yourself - just barely hanging on to life, feeling you are about to fall into the dark abyss at any moment?

Many salespeople find themselves losing their balance regardless of where they are on the spectrum of life, whether they are poor performers or compulsive workaholics.

Both types would emphatically state that they must find a better way to live and work.

52 Living a Balanced Life

In the old days, people just lived their lives, not giving much thought to their daily routines. Daily opportunities and challenges fully occupied them from the moment they arose until they collapsed in their beds. But somewhere along the way, we began to pay attention to the concept of balance in life. Books were written, talk-show pundits espoused it, spouses and kids started requiring it, and before you knew it, balance became one more thing every salesperson needs to attend to. Oh yeah!

Being balanced is not so onerous. When you are living and working *On Purpose*, every day blends activities and events that are connected to who you are as a person, whether you are at work, at play, or at home. Living the balanced life starts with being On Purpose, both personally and professionally. You must choose where and how you exert your time and talent. This takes discipline, because you face countless choices and not all are healthy.

Salespeople live in a virtual world, often operating out of a home office in a spare bedroom. They spend hours on countless conference calls, begging and bartering for company resources for their customers and prospects, while trying to get face-to-face with the contacts who will help them achieve their sales quotas.

They have to get all of that done before their daughter's soccer game, their son's karate lesson – and then chair the fundraising committee meeting for the community project someone convinced them to support.

And on top of that, balanced people are bound and determined to reserve some quiet time for the loves of their lives, the reason why they do all they do, day in, day out, in the first place.

Just as you do not achieve sales mastery instantly, neither do you achieve perfect life balance in a day. Don't try to do everything at once. Rather, periodically take the time to review your total work and personal life. Assess what's working and what's not – give yourself progress reports. Make adjustments as needed.

Ah, isn't life grand and fulfilling! Balance is all about journeys, not destinations.

53 👎 Not Real: Living on the Run

As we've seen, many people get into the profession of selling by accident, often because there are more positions available in sales than in almost any other profession. How many actually chose sales as their life's work? Whether they sell cars or computers, what caused them to gravitate to this calling? And is selling truly a career for them? Or is it just a way to make enough money to put food on the table, keep a roof over the family's heads, put clothes on their backs, and hopefully put a few bucks in the bank to save for a rainy day?

Some people get into sales to give themselves time to figure out what they really want to do. They start to make enough money to get by, often finding themselves drifting from one sales job to another. They believe that with each change, the new job is going to be the big one! Yet, they end up not feeling any more secure, productive, or rewarded.

There's another large contingent of salespeople who truly do make it big. They live in comfort, pay their bills and sock money away for their kids' college education, pursue their hobbies and sports, socialize, make global getaways every year, and think they have really made it to the good life!

These two groups, even though they live at opposite ends of the salesperson spectrum, have a few things in common, but in different dimensions. Both groups live on the edge, on the one hand in a world of fear and scarcity, and in the other, of maintaining a high-cost lifestyle and risk. And whether it is the edge close to poverty or to materialistic overload, life for both can feel empty. Or to put it differently: one feels the thrill of the hunt, the other the fear of being hunted!

At some point, those who find themselves in the sales profession must ask themselves these questions when they look in the mirror, regardless if they are alone or on the world stage: Why do I do what I do? What do I really want to do – in this job, in this company, in this world?

Am I living on the run?

Or...

Am I living On Purpose?

54 Living On Purpose – Sales as My *Profession*

We have spoken about *living On Purpose*. What do we really mean?

Living On Purpose means seeing and living out the connections between the purpose of your work and the purpose of your life. It is the sum of your daily routines and actions that demonstrate that you want to be significant and do meaningful things.

For the sales professional, living On Purpose involves three essential components:

1. Giving service: giving yourself to a cause or mission larger than yourself. By helping others get what they want, you can get results that you want as well.
2. Using unique talents: the competition most likely offers virtually the same products and features. It is your uniqueness that gives you your competitive edge.
3. Solving problems: it calls on you to devote your career to using your talents to solve problems, whether they are your customers', your community's, or your family's.

This sets up a wonderful paradox. A friend put it well: "I have more fun and enjoy more personal success when I stop trying to get what I want and start helping other people get what they want."

Five elements distinguish salespeople who live in ways that express and clarify their purpose:

1. They accept circumstances: seeing problems as opportunities and focusing on what can be changed and improved by using their talents and trust.
2. They let their Purpose guide them: making a contribution, making a difference.
3. They have goals: specific and tangible ones that can be visualized and measured.

4. They live with a positive attitude: they don't feel restricted by limitations but instead act with determination and focus.
5. They understand commitment: persevering when tough challenges occur, reaching down for strength, and believing in themselves and others.

Finally, living On Purpose requires you to be very clear about what your core beliefs and values are and having the personal and moral courage to cling to them, especially in times of challenge, doubt, and temptation.

Living On Purpose is summed up well by George Bernard Shaw's observation: "This is the true joy in life – being used for a purpose you recognize as a mighty one."

55 👎 Not Real: Surviving vs. Thriving – Settling for Mediocrity

Our friend, author and speaker David McNally, is widely respected for helping individuals break through self-imposed barriers to achieving significant, sustainable success in both their personal and professional lives. A key concept in his approach focuses on the difference between *thrivers* vs. *survivors*. Let's explore how this concept applies to the sales profession.

Many people start work in sales because they have not yet figured out what they want to be when they grow up. You have probably heard at least one fellow salesperson say, "I'll just take this sales job until I find something better to do." Some thrive and advance. For others, before they know it, months, years, and decades have passed and they are still in the same position, most likely with a résumé that shows they keep moving from company to company, schlepping products and services as a way of eking out a living.

Their performance usually speaks for itself. They complain about their quota, without ever buying into or taking responsibility for setting their own goals. They struggle to meet their monthly, quarterly, and yearly sales targets, and sit in the audience at their annual sales meetings every year watching the high performers take the stage, the glory, and the money!

Often they bluff, talking up a good story about a big deal they are working on. Then, when it falls through, they blame their lackluster results on the company, the boss, the economy, the product, and the customer, but never themselves. They simply accept mediocrity as their fate. Unfortunately, this lack of drive may surface in other aspects of their lives as well. They settle for just getting by, for being average, at least in their sales endeavors.

56 Driving Unrelentingly for Sales Results

Real, consummate sales professionals are able to consistently achieve and even exceed their sales plans, year after year. They are the salespeople recognized at every annual sales conference as one of the top performers. So how does a top sales professional make it happen?

Recently we interviewed one of these stars, Gary Weber of Aurora Casket Company, and he boiled the many reasons for his consistent success down to three critical success factors:

1. He works incredibly hard – and works smart.
2. He builds and sustains professional relationships.
3. He focuses on his customers' business issues.

Certainly Gary does other things that contribute to his success. For example, we know that Gary is a superb consultative sales executive, and he is also meticulous in his portfolio management and territory planning. So let's explore some other characteristics besides these critical success factors that can lead you to consistently high performance:

1. Top performers set their own goals and performance standards. Their company-assigned goal is just a way station along the path to their higher personal achievement goal.
2. They push themselves by seeking out challenging assignments. In the words of Robert Kennedy, "There are those that look at things the way they are, and ask *why?* I dream of things that never were, and ask *why not?*"
3. They are committed to learning the skills, using the tools of our trade, and being meticulous in all planning and preparation. According to Vince Lombardi, "Practice does not make perfect; perfect practice makes perfect." The same concept can be said of preparation.
4. They constantly assess and reassess their situation with each customer and use the three tenets of S.E.L. to drive success. Through this analysis

of self and sales, they overcome mistakes and setbacks quickly.

5. They have an unflappable, unwavering will to persevere and win, pushing themselves and their teams to the highest levels of achievement. They really believe there is no glory in anything but first place. All true sales professionals hate to lose; their distaste for losing is often stronger than their will to win.

Top sales performers share an undeniable thirst to perform at the highest levels imaginable. They are driven by passion for results that speak for themselves, yet guided by important skills and techniques that *all* sales professionals can adopt. Being the best of the best – now that's Thriving!

57 Living On Purpose Self-Survey

David McNally, a recognized author and speaker on the practice of living life On Purpose, crafted a tool that helps you assess the extent to which you are living *On Purpose* today.

Give yourself two points if you answer yes, one point if you're not sure, and zero if you answer no. Note that there are no right or wrong answers. The goal is to help you gauge your current status on the On Purpose scale of life.

Questions	Your Score
1. Do you recognize what you are good at? (Of all your skills, which do you enjoy using most?)	2
2. Do you fully utilize those skills?	2
3. Does your work further some interest or issue that you care deeply about?	2
4. Do you see yourself as making a difference in the world through your work?	2
5. Do you view most days with a sense of enthusiasm (vs. as an economic chore)?	2
6. Have you developed your own philosophy of life and success?	2
7. Are you taking the necessary risks to live your philosophy?	2
8. Do you feel a sense of meaning and purpose in your life?	2
9. Do you have active goals relating to your Purpose?	2
10. Are you living your life now (vs. hoping that life will work out someday)?	2
Your Total Score	20

Interpretation

0 – 7 points = You risk not reaching your potential. You may be in a crisis or transition mode temporarily. But you should reassess your sense of your Purpose and direction.

8 – 15 points = You have a sense of Purpose, but need to clarify things, develop your sense of commitment, check whether you are walking your talk.

16 - 20 points = Your way of living is On Purpose to a good extent – you are focused, have a sense of direction, and you may already be making a difference.

58 Concluding Thoughts

As you sit on the plane, or in your office, or on the beach reading this book, we ask you to look around you. Soak in the fact that virtually *everything* around you (save for the sunshine and those waves lapping up on the beach) had to be sold by a sales professional. Furniture, buildings, telephone systems, computers, wireless networks, the chair you sit in – *everything* had to be sold!

Our world commerce would grind to a screeching halt without sales professionals. We are essential to business and society. This vital importance is one of the main reasons why we call sales a truly noble profession.

The other reason is that it truly is the most non-discriminatory role in society. It is a role that, at its core, is only concerned with performance. No matter if you are black, white, man, woman, or you come from a rich or dirt-poor background, sales performance is blind, like justice. All that matters in the challenging, rewarding world of professional selling is that you are a problem-solving, empathetic person who improves other people's worlds with the solutions you bring them.

Sales is not an easy job. It is not for everyone. You must be prepared for great adversity. You will not survive if you are not supremely competitive. The profession of selling requires an amazing skill set that is part consultant, part business manager, part accountant, and part psychologist.

The rewards that can come from this wonderfully difficult profession are beyond the dreams of many. Both of us came from extremely humble beginnings. Michael Boland grew up in the small community of Frog Hollow, Pennsylvania (just outside of Pittsburgh, Pennsylvania), happily oblivious to much of the world beyond. Over the course of his career he has personally led a global sales force, traveling around the world. He rose to lead a powerful consulting firm that has thrived for nearly thirty years on the simple concept of teaching sales professionals to be all that they can be. Keith Hawk grew up across the street from a pig farm in the tiny community of Sabina, Ohio. He rose through the sales ranks to lead a thousand-plus person sales organization in one of America's most high-tech industries, and he speaks all over the world on the Real sales principles we've described in this book.

We tell you this not to brag. Rather, we tell you to ask you to dream – to dream about how great your life can become if you commit yourself to the concept that *you are a Real sales professional!* If you commit to the techniques and processes we've presented here, we are highly confident that your life can be changed for the better forever.

We want to hear from you. Start your journey of personal development. Become the best sales professional in your company. We dream of standing on-stage at your company's top performer award ceremony, shaking your hand, looking into your eyes. We will give you the nod of understanding that can only be grasped by Real sales professionals.

Good Luck! God Bless you!

Keith Hawk   Michael Boland

Appendix A: **The Get-Real Sales Call Planner**

Use the questions and tips on this page and the worksheet on the next to prepare for a productive Discovery meeting with a client.

What is your Ben Duffy introduction? (See page 57.) • Prepare information about yourself, your company, and how you do business with your customer in mind. Imagine questions the customer might have; share those questions with the customer; confirm that they match, or add to or modify yours as needed. Then answer the questions. This reduces relationship tension and demonstrates that you are an empathetic person who has the customer's best interests in mind. Remember your S.E.L. purpose and vividly demonstrate that you believe "My success can only follow the success of my customer."	
Prepare your Purpose – Process – Payoff statements. • What do we hope to accomplish as we work together today? (Purpose) • How will we work when we are together? (Process) • What possible gains can be made for the customer and us from the meeting? (Payoff)	

What will you ask in Discovery?
 • The Magic Question: "What are those few things that absolutely must go right for you to achieve your most important business priorities?" Then follow up with these:
   - "What specific plans do you have in place to assure that these priorities are achieved?"
   - "Who is most responsible for achieving each of these plans?"
   - "What are the most serious anticipated obstacles and challenges to the success of these plans?"	

Is there an in-place competitor already doing business with this customer? • If yes, what is my strategy to supplant the competitor? (Direct? Indirect? Segment? Reposition?) What relationships do we have within the organization?	
What executives in the firm do we need to meet to understand the key business priorities and to understand who will be involved in each priority from an standpoint?	

Initial Discovery Planning Tool

Company name: Contact name and title:

Date of meeting: Location of meeting:

Ben Duffy Questions:	
Purpose Process Payoff	
S.E.L. Statements	
Magic Question: What few things must absolutely go right for your business to achieve its most important business priorities?	
Follow-up: What plans do you have in place to achieve each of these priorities?	
Task motives: Personal motives:	
Action items from this meeting:	

Appendix B:

The Get-Real Skills and Practices Checklist

Use this checklist to refresh yourself on the key points in this book.

❏ *S.E.L.* – My success can only follow the success of my customers. As a sales professional I am always seeking to help them in three ways:

1. Service – Through my solutions I will help my customer provide better service to *his customers.*
2. Economics – I will provide solutions that positively impact the economics of my customers' organization, either through raising their revenues or helping them to reduce expenses.
3. Life – Through my solutions the quality of work life of my customer and his employees will be improved.

❏ *Solutions Selling* – Creating sales opportunities by discovering the most important priorities in my customer's business and helping him achieve those priorities with my company's solutions. I am not just selling *a product.* Rather, I am finding ways to solve difficult problems by assembling *a solution.*

❏ *Don't Be a Bag Diver* – The misled sales person who constantly dives into his virtual bag of products, pitching them at the customer in the mode of "Stop me when you're ready to buy something." The Bag Diver always focuses on features, prices, and the current promotion. He is a human brochure.

❏ *Differentiation* – The road to competitive success is to discover how you and your company can do a better job than all others through the unique differences that you and your solutions can bring to the customer. The thinking sales professional can differentiate on service, product, company commitment, relationship, problem-solving approach, pricing creativity, and many other elements. Enhance your business acumen by spending 20 minutes each day reading about the world of business. There are a host of superb online publications that can make this easy and fun (see Chapter 15).

❏ *Work your current accounts* – The greatest source of new business is often found within your existing accounts. Make sure that you protect and grow these crown jewels of your company. It is more difficult to open and develop a new account than it is to keep and grow a current one.

❏ *Manage your interactions* – It is vital that you reduce relationship tension early in a new business relationship. We do this by sharing our S.E.L. approach and by giving crystal clear descriptions of why we are meeting today and how we will work when we are together. Remember to utilize Wilson Learning's Ben Duffy technique and "Purpose-Process-Payoff" in your customer interactions.

❏ *Discovery* – This process is the cornerstone to sales success. You must take the time and effort to discover your customer's business plans and challenges. You must discover *those few things that absolutely must go right* within your customer's business. These individual discoveries will lead to your ultimate solution offering that you will present to your customer.

❏ *Strategize* – Successful sales executives apply strategy at three levels:

- Account Management
- Opportunity Management
- Sales Call Management

❏ *Proposals* – Use a consciously competent process and order for presenting your solution:

- Purpose-Process-Payoff
- Current State
- Description of the Solution
- Ask for questions
- Implementation plan
- The Close – just a "dot" in the sales process

❏ *Call high* – It is important to call on executives, as they can provide guidance and help you understand the true priorities of their business. There are special things you can do that they value. Focus on discovering those few things that absolutely must go right when you meet with top business leaders.

❏ *Forecasting* – You should not kid yourself or your company with your forecasts. We advocate a simple "opportunity board" that shows where you are in the sales process with each of your active accounts and prospects.

❏ *Metrics* – You must discover the metrics that matter in your business. Though we often think the only numbers that matter are our final sales results, there are other indicators that lead to our results. You must become keenly aware of these metrics and track them as you manage your own success. The end results are merely our "scoreboard," not the true indicators of what leads to your success as a sales professional.

❏ *Be both a Hunter and a Farmer* – Great sales professionals have healthy doses of both Hunter and Farmer in their personal makeup. They understand the value of always seeking new opportunities while tending to the importance of protecting and harvesting their existing customer base.

❏ *Live and work On Purpose* – The skills you develop as a Real sales professional can help you in other important aspects of your life. Seeing yourself as a problem-solver will spill over into your life outside work and give you added satisfaction there as well. We find we have more fun and enjoy more personal success when we stop trying to get what we want and start helping other people get what they want.

❏ *Sales is a truly noble profession* – The world of commerce would grind to a halt were it not for the work that we do! On the next page you'll find another planning tool that can help you really apply everything you've been reading about in this book. Success!

Presentation Planning Tool

Company name: Contact name and title:

Date of meeting: Location of meeting:

Purpose Process Payoff	
Review key discovery findings	
S.E.L. statements	
Solution Advantage Benefits	
Closing statements	
Implementation: next steps	

Bibliography

Bistritz, Steve. Renowned resource for strategic sales competencies. Has contributed several articles in *The Journal of Selling and Major Account Management* and wrote the article, "Effectively Assessing Sales Opportunities: The Continuing Dilemma for Today's Sales Managers." Founder of Learning Solutions International.

Bund, Barbara. *Winning and Keeping Industrial Customers: The Dynamics of Customer Relationships* (Lexington Books). We acknowledge Bund's development of the Account Behavior Spectrum model and her studies of lasting and non-lasting vendor-supplier relationships.

McNally, David. *The Eagle's Secret* (Dell Publishing). McNally provides inspiration for the millennium – strategies to help you soar to new heights of personal achievement no matter how far you have to fly! Be ready to work – and love it – as you begin a journey of self-discovery that leads to a confident new vision of career and life.

McNally, David. *The Power of Purpose*. In this award-winning documentary film, McNally speaks to five specific elements that help clarify your own sense of purpose: Acceptance, Purpose, Goals, Attitude, and Commitment.

Miller, William "Skip." *Proactive Sales Management* (AMACOM). Miller breaks the sales rep's and sales manager's roles down into meaningful pieces, and he is very tactical. We like that and hope that you will view *Get-Real Selling* in the same way.

Misner, Ivan R. and Don Morgan. *Masters of Sales: Secrets from Top Sales Professionals that Will Transform You into a World-Class Salesperson* (Entrepreneur Media). A highly tactical book taken from the top selling practices of some of the world's greatest practitioners.

Mulch, Steve. Master at the art of engaging new contacts for securing appointments and monitoring sales process through successful completion. Founder of Veritas Training.

Parinello, Anthony, *Selling To VITO* (Adams Media Corporation). Offers innovative ideas and street-smart tactics for reaching the Very Important Top Officer in any organization.

Richardson, Linda. *Sales Coaching: Making the Great Leap from Sales Manager to Sales Coach* (McGraw-Hill). We share Richardson's point of view that truly great sales managers must constantly fulfill their primary role: coach, not manager.

Schiffman, Stephan. *The 25 Sales Skills They Don't Teach at Business School*. (Adams Media Corporation). We are big fans of Schiffman's work. He is a prolific author and sales trainer who simplifies sales processes and techniques. We are especially keen on his sales-prospect management process.

Tzu, Sun and James Clavell. *The Art of War* (Delacorte Press). A classic. Sun Tzu was a philosopher before he ever became a general, and he discusses all aspects of war, from the tactical to the human. James Clavell takes Tzu's precepts and applies them to today's world – the world of business as well as daily life.

Ury, William. *Getting to Yes* (Penguin Books). Offers a concise, step-by-step, proven strategy for coming to mutually acceptable agreements in every sort of negotiation, especially in selling.

Ury, William. *Getting Past No* (Bantam Books). Offers a proven breakthrough strategy for turning adversaries into negotiating partners.

Wilson, Larry. Larry is the pioneer in consultative selling and a master of effective customer interaction. Founder of Wilson Learning Corporation, premier provider of sales and leadership training. Books include: *Play to Win!; Changing the Game; Stop Selling, Start Partnering; The One Minute Salesperson.*

Wilson Learning Library, *Versatile Selling* (Nova Vista Publishing). Versatility is a powerful, yet simple way to treat customers the way they want to be treated. It gets you and the customer to "Yes!" sooner by leveraging the human side of the sale.

Wilson Learning Library. *Win-Win Selling* (Nova Vista Publishing). More than a million people in companies all around the world have adopted Wilson Learning's Counselor approach to selling. Models, cases, techniques, tips, and tools make it a valuable book for beginning and experienced salespeople.

About the Authors

Keith Hawk is a 29-year veteran sales professional and sales leader. Over the course of his career he has developed a rich understanding of what it takes to be a successful sales professional. For over ten years he led one of America's greatest sales organizations, at LexisNexis. He continues in a customer-focused role to this day at that global organization, speaking to customer groups around the world on the topic of solving business problems with the solutions offered by his firm. In addition, he continues to lecture regularly on topics such as consultative selling, selling to executives, and his personal favorite: the true role of the sales professional.

Keith is married and has three sons. He loves watching his sons play professional football and being a new grandparent. Youngest son A.J. Hawk is a linebacker with the NFL's Green Bay Packers. Middle son Ryan was a quarterback at Ohio University and in the Arena2 professional football league. Eldest son Matthew and his wife Beth have thrilled Keith and his wife Judy with two grandchildren.

Michael Boland has 36 years of experience in sales and sales leadership. He founded Performance Technologies in 1982, a business consulting and training firm, which specializes in helping its customers WIN by developing elite sales forces led by exceptional coaches. As a business consultant, Michael's strength lies in his ability to distill complex issues into workable solutions and to lead organizations through transformation that converts challenges into achievement.

Michael is married to his high school sweetheart Emilee, and they revel in the lives of their adult children and especially all of their grandchildren. He is devoted to his parish and religious community and contributes his leadership and voice to the pro-life movement in his local and state organizations.

E-mail Keith and Michael at: getreal@performancetec.com

Index

91,067.29
2500.00
8250.00
2500.00
500.00

3667.00
12833.00

24.00
17,378.65
3850.00
3526.00
80.00
158,256.16

Half UMG -waived
11,419.71
2500

C&S

2500
2596
1531.25
5502.91
8913.39
2540.00
106,233.01
56.00
1250.00
32.00
122.00
1000.00
40.00
1039.14
6533.22
30.00
108.75
2355.92
399,885.54
46,356.22

What would you do
if you were in my position?

ONE SIZE DOES not fit all

1. Strategize –
   – Subject matter expert CSG on call –
     3 big circus
   (only work w/ SCS?
   ask off topic questions?
   (– Economist
     → NARRATIVE Response

2. Issues into OPP –   Friday 45 mm
   go on Data Collection

3. Role – Stay involved but don't overwhelme CSG
     or Data Collector
   – Lawyers that don't want to deal w this
     need to use you

4. Finding the Whale –
   – everything about the kill
   → never give credit to an CSM or
     two level associate

5. Act's a Reporter
   – Circle givens, funny anecdotes
     don't be smug to add value.
   – only on calls
     Self depricating humor.
   – Be well founded –

6.) Envision where you want to be
    learn from the best